How to Audition for the Musical Theatre

A STEP-BY-STEP GUIDE TO EFFECTIVE PREPARATION

Revised Edition

Donald Oliver

Drama Book Publishers
New York

No practitioner of the arts can survive without a nurturing environment. I am blessed with a large, warm, wise, loving, and unshakably supportive family. It is to all of them that I dedicate this book; but most especially to Rosalind Oliver, my aunt, and the memory of Bernard Oliver, my beloved uncle.

782.81071
OL34
146164
Mar. 1989

LIBRARY OF CONGRESS
Library of Congress Cataloging-in-Publication Data

Oliver, Donald.
    How to audition for the musical theatre: a step-by-step guide to effective preparation / Donald Oliver.—Rev. ed.
         p.   cm.
    ISBN 0-89676-101-0
    1. Singing—Auditions. 2. Music—Performance. I. Title.
MT892.04 1988
782.81'07'1—dc 19   88-20241
                                                    CIP
                                                    MN

ACKNOWLEDGEMENTS

Both as a professional and personal colleague, director Bill Gile played an important role in my developing many of the ideas in this book. So I take this opportunity to thank him, not only for all the times he hired me as an audition accompanist, which allowed these theories to develop, but also for his advice and opinions as this manuscript took shape. I was also fortunate to have received guidance early on from the extraordinary pianist and composer Sande Campbell—her comments and recommendations have been freely incorporated in the text and I am in her debt.

I am also deeply appreciative of those people who took the time to share their helpful ideas and audition stories: Jeanie Breall, Mary Jo Catlett, Morton DaCosta, Jeffrey Dunn, Rob Fisher, Paul Ford, Jerry Herman, Sheldon Harnick, John Kander, James Kirkwood, Jack Lee, Edward Strauss, and Peter Wandel.

It was one thing to gather all these ideas; it was quite another to write them down in an organized fashion. And so I was lucky to have received the editorial help of Phillipa Keil and Judith Holmes.

One last thank-you goes to David Spencer for his keen comments on the final manuscript. This book has benefited from his acute observations and suggestions.

CONTENTS

Acknowledgements iii

The Explanation Department 1

All About Auditions 4

    The Casting Team 9

    The Interactive Elements of an Audition 11

    Audition Announcements: The Trade Papers 18

PREPARATION — Part I: Selecting

Where to Find an Accompanist 25

Your Audition Repertoire 27

    Building a Song Portfolio 28

What Not to Sing 33

Where to Find Songs 39

PREPARATION — Part II: The Mechanics

How to Prepare Your Music 47

    Transposition 50

    Professional Copying 51

    The Care and Feeding of Your Music 52

Interpretation: Acting the Song 56

Working with a Vocal Coach 60

PREPARATION — Part III: Performing

When to Bring Your Own Pianist 67

Singing the Right Kind of Song 70

At the Audition: Do's and Don't's
    Hints and Secrets   72
How to Talk to a Pianist
    And What to Say   79
What to Do if You Forget the Lyrics   81
The Open Call   83
Summer Stock   85
At the Callback   87
A Touch of the Outrageous   89
After the Audition   92

APPENDICES
APPENDIX A: A Partial List of the Most
                Overdone Audition Songs   97
APPENDIX B: Excuses, Excuses   101
APPENDIX C: Taping Your Music   103
APPENDIX D: Your Photo and Resume   105
APPENDIX E: To Agent or Not to Agent (And
                Other Questions Answered)   108
APPENDIX F: Advice to the Personal Accompanist   115
APPENDIX G: Helpful Names and Addresses   116
LAGNIAPPE: My Favorite Audition Story   122
ABOUT THE AUTHOR   123

THE EXPLANATION DEPARTMENT

This is a manual on how to prepare for a musical audition—and how to present yourself and your talent in the best possible light at the audition itself.

Over the course of the last thirteen years I have played the piano for literally thousands of auditions. It has always amazed me how many talented people make similar mistakes while auditioning, diminishing their chances of being seriously considered, while some performers with less natural ability make the absolute most of their potential—and get the jobs.

From all this I have come to the somewhat less-than-earth-shattering conclusion that if you have your act together, it *is* possible to weight auditions in your favor by minimizing the risks.

This book will lay out the proper guidelines. Although geared primarily for people new to the business, it should be helpful to performers at any stage of their career. If an actor or actress is just starting out, following the advice herein can make him or her seem to be a seasoned professional at their very first audition. Those experienced at auditioning will find much useful information, especially if they are constantly auditioning and not getting jobs. As you will see, there's usually a reason for that, and the solution to the problem can be found between these covers.

ALL ABOUT AUDITIONS

Can you remember the moment you first decided to pursue a career in the musical theatre? Was it when you had a solo in a school show and heard the audience applaud you for the first time? Was it when your favorite relative heard you sing or saw you dance and said you were every bit as good as anyone already on the New York stage? Or did you get bitten when you saw a certain movie or live show—perhaps a touring company—and afterwards, exhilarated, you proclaimed to all who would listen, "That's what I want to do!"

Well, congratulations! You have picked a field that is simultaneously demanding, competitive, frustrating, and glamorous. Always remember that show business is a *business,* filled with myths and misconceptions, legends and lore. Within this most changeable and unreliable of professions there is only one constant: an unbelievably high rate of unemployment—over 80 percent at any given time. Almost all struggling performers are forced to work at decidedly unglamorous jobs in order to support themselves while waiting for opportunities to display their craft in public.

So before I go into the actual step-by-step discussion on how to select and prepare your audition material, it's important to explore some of the realities of the industry, answer some questions, and clue you in as to what tools-of-the-trade you'll need to begin.

Since you have this idea that you'd like to sing and dance on Broadway someday, you'll have to let those people who can make your dream come true know you're alive and kicking. You'll have to attend auditions.

An audition is an event at which performers desirous of being part of a production demonstrate their talent to the people who will make casting decisions. First the auditioner will sing. Then, if his singing is found acceptable, he may be asked to read aloud a scene from the show, possibly in tandem with someone else auditioning the same day.*

If the membership of Actors' Equity (the union for theatrical stage performers) were polled, it would most likely be found that a full 95 percent of them really don't like auditioning. Nor do the people who must evaluate auditions much like the process. But so far no one has found a more effective system for viewing and evaluating talent.

The process of auditioning has many drawbacks. For one, actors are performing without costumes, makeup, or proper lighting—hardly optimal circumstances.

And, for two, most are nervous.

With good reason. An audition is the show-business version of a job interview. In a very short amount of time, actors have to perform a mini-commercial, and the product they are hawking is *themselves*. One young man was so nervous at his audition that

---

* The subject of audition-readings can, and does, take up a book of its own, the best being the one by Michael Shurtleff mentioned in my preface.

as he was singing the song "Oklahoma!," he spelled it, "O-K-L-M-N . . ."

A lot of people don't realize that an audition can represent only one of several appearances before the people doing the hiring. Casting their show is a serious enterprise for the creative team, so they reserve the right to have you audition for them on more than one occasion. These return visits are termed "callbacks."

The excitement of being called back for a second or a third hearing doesn't make actors any less nervous than they were the first time. The pressure increases as the stakes become higher.

The fallibility of the whole audition process produces many unfortunate situations. There are marvelously talented performers who are capable and inventive in a rehearsal or performance situation, but who just don't audition well; and there are reverse-performers who audition brilliantly but don't live up to their potential when cast.

But *everyone*—including any star you can name—has had to audition at one time or another in his career.

Barbra Streisand auditioned for Eddie Blum of the Rodgers and Hammerstein casting office when *The Sound of Music* was on Broadway. She sang for three hours, hoping to take over the featured role of Liesl—who sings "Sixteen Going on Seventeen." Afterwards, she was given much encouragement by Mr. Blum but was told she wasn't right for anything in *The Sound Of Music*. The lucky one here was Mr. Blum, who was the recipient of a free, private, three-hour Barbra Streisand concert.

Even a performer as gifted as John Travolta had to learn the basics of auditioning. While performing in an Off-Broadway production of *Rain,* a nonmusical play, he was asked to audition for the prestigious Goodspeed Opera House in Connecticut.

According to witnesses, he apparently hadn't been previously coached in the *mechanics* of a musical audition. Not being prepared to sing with a live pianist, he brought a cassette recorder with him—his musical accompaniment was on tape—and when he sang, he was not quite in sync with the recording. Extremely nervous, he made a bad showing, and couldn't convince the producer of his potential worth. Now at that time, he was merely one of many performers who auditioned for Goodspeed and didn't make it. But he didn't let it discourage him; he kept at it and learned what he didn't know. Soon thereafter he landed important roles in the Broadway shows *Grease* and *Over Here!*, which led directly to his exciting television and movie career.

It should be clear that it takes guts to audition at any stage in your career. Here are three more stories that tell about star performers with guts; coincidentally, each story has to do with Jerry Herman's musicals. Remember as you read—at the time these incidents took place, none of the three shows mentioned were the celebrated, wildly successful, award-winning musicals we now know them to be.

Carol Channing has been a star since 1949 when she played Lorelei Lee in *Gentlemen Prefer Blondes* and introduced the song "Diamonds Are A Girl's Best Friend." In 1963 she had to audition for *Hello, Dolly!* Why? Because the role of Dolly would be a departure for her from Lorelei Lee and the other kinds of roles she had been associated with. She was neither offended nor afraid—she knew what she had to offer, and she understood that the production team needed to be convinced she had the particular quality they were looking for. She went on to win the 1964 Tony Award for Best Actress in a Musical. Just for the record, her competition that year was none other than Barbra Streisand in *Funny Girl;* Beatrice Lillie in *High Spirits;* and Inga Swenson in *110 in the Shade*.

In 1965, when the musical *Mame* was looking for its leading lady, Angela Lansbury had already been nominated for three Academy Awards. Every major female star at that time was either considered for or approached to play Mame. Everyone from Judy Garland to Ethel Merman to Mary Martin. Everyone but Angela Lansbury. Ms. Lansbury, who had starred in the musical *Anyone Can Whistle* on Broadway the year before, came to New York on her own and auditioned. But on the day of her audition the only one of *Mame*'s creators she impressed was its composer-lyricist, Jerry Herman. Afterwards, without the knowledge of the producers or director, Mr. Herman secretly taught her "If He Walked Into My Life," the stunning song from the score, and arranged for a second audition at which he played the piano, accompanying her. We all know now about Ms. Lansbury's subsequent triumph in the show, but at the time it was very brave on her part to go along with the second audition, because it could've gone the other way. She too, as did Ms. Channing, won a Tony Award, beating out Gwen Verdon in *Sweet Charity;* Julie Harris in *Skyscraper;* and Barbara Harris in *On A Clear Day You Can See Forever.*

La Cage aux Folles was a show for which auditions were mandatory, especially for stars. The requirements for the leading roles were so unique that the previous work of any actor wasn't enough to show the creators exactly what they needed for their leads. George Hearn was a much respected, hard-working, versatile actor with an off-stage reputation as an accomplished lothario, who, prior to 1983, never even *fantasized* about dressing in women's clothing. But he wanted to play the role of Albin in *La Cage,* and with absolutely no guarantees that it would turn out positively, he had the courage to agree to have Ted Azar—*La Cage*'s very talented hair and makeup designer—help him get completely done up in female attire for his audition. In drag, Mr. Hearn marched onto the stage, sang "My Heart Belongs To Daddy," and the part was his. He showed the production team that he had the theatrical guts they needed for *La Cage*. When he accepted *his* Tony Award, he pointed to it and said, "What some people won't do . . ."

THE CASTING TEAM

For a moment, let's look at things from the point of view of those casting the show.

The creative team has to see and seriously consider sometimes up to 100 people a day for several days in a row. They have to remember who was good, who was not, who should be seen again for the current production, and who may be useful at some later time—all the while trying to impartially compare the relative abilities of everyone who auditions.

This is neither an easy nor an enviable task. Since a shocking number of performers are ill-prepared to audition—in ways which are fully described in this book—their allotted moments in front of the people they're supposed to impress is a waste of time for both parties. And the hours spent watching that certain percentage of auditioners whose talent is not readily discernible is a valuable chunk of time most creative people could use doing other necessary preproduction work. But they have to cast their show by enduring the rigors of the audition process so these built-in problems are all part of the the game.

While they are planning (or creating) the production, the creative team usually has a pretty good idea of what they're looking for in their future cast members. If they are even the slightest bit uncertain about the ideal physical look of the characters, they know the fairly inflexible (and in some cases pretty well impossible) technical requirements for the roles. When you stand before the casting team they long for you to be the answer to their prayers because they can relax only when someone appears who is perfect for their needs.

In a conversation with me, composer John Kander (*Cabaret, Chicago, The Rink*) underscored the fact that the people judging an audition really do want you to be good when you step out in front of them because they have to cast all the roles in their show—except, sometimes, the star parts—from the people who audition. Jerry Herman said, "We're really nice guys who want to hire everybody. It's painful to see talented people walk by and not be able to use them."

Director Morton DaCosta (*Auntie Mame, The Music Man*) told me that at auditions he suffers as much as the people who are auditioning. Having first been an actor—most directors and choreographers started out as performers—he has firsthand knowledge of what people go through.

Because of the stakes, the members of the creative team are often just as nervous and apprehensive as you are. Mr. Kander remembers an incident during the casting of his show *The Happy Time,* when someone auditioning had an unusually large nose. The late Gower Champion, who directed and choreographed the show, was well known for his kindness and consideration during his auditions. Mr. Champion and the authors felt so sorry for this particular performer that, although pressed for time, they allowed a complete song to be sung and were overly solicitous afterward. In an ill-fated attempt at graciousness, Mr. Champion jumped out of his seat in the theatre and rushed up onto the stage where he said, "Thank you, that was very *nose.*"

Actors often gripe that "the same people get hired over and over, and newcomers don't have a chance." That is not true by design. All directors and writers are excited by the possibility of discovering fresh talent at an audition. There is a certain kind of thrill that comes when an actor or actress unknown to the production team displays the talent and the vitality necessary for the show.

Please believe that finding and developing new performers is sort of an unofficial mission of everyone connected with the theatre. Like Dracula's, the theatre's only hope of survival is through continually replenishing the supplies of fresh blood.

THE INTERACTIVE ELEMENTS OF AN AUDITION

Many complex factors come into play during an audition. You are judged by the subtle interplay of the following elements:

1. YOUR "LOOK"

In other words, how close you come to the author's or director's *physical* concept of the role. If they're set on a blonde and you're a brunette, you probably have very little chance of changing their minds. However, and here's where the interactive nature of the audition process shows itself, your strengths in any of the other areas talked about later *can* make a difference.

Try to get an accurate gauge of what "type" you are. Are you the "handsome, strong, leading man" or "beautiful leading lady" type? Or does your face and figure suggest a "character" type? Do you look your age? Younger? Older? Can you vary your look to expand your suitable age range?

You must come up with HONEST answers to the above questions and, at the same time, be ruthless about any positive changes you may be able to affect in your appearance. For example, if you are overweight and perceive yourself as the leading man or leading lady type, you'd be well advised to shed the extra poundage immediately. Think about it: How frequently do you see an obviously chubby hero or heroine in the theatre or films? Not often. And even then, how often is the lead's chubbiness not an integral part of the story?

2. YOUR VOICE

This category has to do with the quality of your vocal instrument and your range. If you are a lyric soprano and the score doesn't call for that, you could have the most magnificent voice ever heard by human ears and still not get a callback.

It is imperative that women develop a "chest voice" as well as a "head voice"—with proper training, both techniques can be used without hurting your throat. Remember: the more versatile you are, the greater are your chances of getting cast.

This may come as a surprise, but you don't have to be an extraordinary singer to get cast in a musical. If you are strong in most of the other areas mentioned in this section, your voice might be "good enough" for the purposes of the show. As will be discussed at length later, you must carefully select songs to sing that show off your voice—whatever your ability—to maximum advantage.

3. YOUR ACTING ABILITY

More on this later in the book. (See Interpretation: Acting the Song.) In brief, having a glorious voice is not enough. You must have something going on behind your eyes. You can't just *sing* your song; you must *act* it as well. In addition to your voice training, you should be attending acting classes and/or scene study workshops. You will never get hired for speaking roles if you can't act. When you open your mouth to sing, people can tell whether or not you can act your way out of that proverbial paper bag.

4. YOUR DANCE ABILITY

All actors are counseled to be as well equipped with the tools of their trade as possible. To this end, I strongly suggest that everyone who wants to be a professional performer in the musical theatre should enroll in some kind of dance class, whether it be ballet, jazz, or tap. Dance training gives people an awareness of and confidence in their bodies, in the way they move, and in the way they look to others. One-line parts in shows—such as, "Telegram for you, Sir,"—are almost always given to dancers rather than to singers simply because dancers are more certain to look graceful crossing the stage. Dance classes are relatively inexpensive—they cost a lot less than vocal coaching—and, at least in New York City, there are so many different classes taking place each day it's easy to find one at a convenient time.

True, to land a lead in a show you don't have to be as proficient a dancer as a chorus gypsy; but if you are called upon to execute a few dance steps as part of a song routine, you won't look graceful without training.

Remember: You can never be too talented—or too skilled. You must be as versatile as possible. The competition is too stiff.

5. YOUR CHOICE OF MATERIAL

A large section of this book is devoted to helping you choose the right material to audition with. Briefly, just as the proper choice of a song can perk up the ears of the listeners and make them react favorably to your talent, the wrong choice can adversely affect your "castability." The casting team writes down what songs you sing, and later, when the inevitable discussion takes place as to whether or not you should be given a callback, you are often remembered chiefly by what song you sang.

6. YOUR APPEARANCE

Although being in show business grants people the right to a certain amount of flamboyance, you should *always* come to an audition dressed as neatly as possible. For men, a jacket and tie is the safest way to go except during hot weather when a clean sport shirt will do adequately. For women, the best outfit is a skirt or dress that is flattering, feminine, and comfortable—no pants, please, unless you look absolutely smashing in them. A little glamour couldn't hurt, but avoid overdressing; don't wear hats or excessive jewelry. Be well groomed with a sensible, as in not-too-trendy, haircut. I realize there are other clothing choices for both men and women that would serve nicely. I am talking about safe, all-purpose dressing.

And now a few words about footwear, ladies first. Please wear attractive shoes which help you move gracefully. Platform shoes are cumbersome and ungainly. Bedroom slippers, no matter how comfortable, are best left under the bed. Buy one good pair of fashionable shoes in a neutral color which can go with many different outfits and only wear them as your "audition shoes." As for the men, although I've seen sneakers and boots look both stylish and flattering, they may not be appropriate for all occasions. You cannot go wrong if you follow my cautious, conservative, middle-of-the-road approach to your appearance. Don't forget what you were told in school: "Neatness counts."

There is one other factor to consider: If you have specific knowledge of the show for which you are auditioning, you may want to choose your clothes by taking into account the age and style of the character for which you will be considered. You do not have to show up in costume—George Hearn was *asked* to dress in drag for his *La Cage aux Folles* audition—but if you are young and the role calls for a more mature performer, dressing appropriately can help you be seen in the right context. Similarly, if you are auditioning for a production of *Les Miserables* or *Fiddler on the Roof,* looking vaguely "peasanty" is better than showing up in smart, tailored clothing.

7. YOUR CREDITS AND EXPERIENCE

This is based, of course, on what appears on your resume. As I mentioned earlier, people are always looking for fresh talent, so an extensive list of credits is not de rigueur if you are right for a particular role. (See Appendix D for more specific advice about the look and content of your resume.)

8. YOUR PERSONALITY

This is arguably the most important variable. And it brings up the single most valuable piece of advice—given to me by a Broadway director—I can give you about auditioning:

You must make the director want to work with you in the first thirty seconds of your audition.

For example, Liliane Montevecchi's role in *Nine* was originally intended for a man, but the lady's personality so dazzled Tommy Tune, the director-choreographer, and Maury Yeston, the composer-lyricist, that after her audition they reconceived the part. Mr. Yeston then wrote the song "Folies Bergères" specifically for her and she went on to win a Tony Award. Similarly, Ben Vereen's Tony Award-winning part in *Pippin* was originally intended for a much older man.

The lesson to be drawn from this is that if you display a knockout package consisting of charm, a sense of humor, a sense of security, and a great measure of talent, the people sitting behind the desk in that audition room are going to notice you. And even if there is no place for you in that particular show, you *will* be remembered for future projects.

Now to confuse matters further, sometimes getting cast has very little to do with any of the above, as exemplified in this amusing story:

James Kirkwood, now the Pulitzer Prize-winning coauthor of *A Chorus Line,* began his career as an actor and nightclub performer. During his stint on the then popular television soap opera *Valiant Lady,* he was informed that he was to audition for Tallulah Bankhead, who was set to star in *Welcome, Darlings,* a summer stock package being created and tailored for her. This show was to include some of the same material from Ms. Bankhead's disastrous edition of the *Ziegfeld Follies,* which closed during its pre-Broadway tryout a few months prior. Mr. Kirkwood was to meet Tallulah at her town house because she did not want to go to a theatre.

He was extremely nervous when he arrived at her home in the East Sixties in Manhattan. She was still getting dressed upstairs, and he could hear her yelling at one of her dogs, "Delores, stop that! Get out of there, Delores!"

Finally, she came down the stairs, picking at her eyelashes. "Hello, darling. I just got up and I always get this garbage in my eyes when I wake up. Do *you* have all of that crap in your eyes when you wake up?" Nonplussed, he answered, "Yes, of course I do."

Peering at him, she said, "James Kirkwood, right? I've seen you on the soap opera. I like you very much; I like your acting. Somebody told me you were a nightclub comic too. What kind of material do you do? Do you have anything you can audition for me now?"

"Actually," he said, dreading the idea of doing his night-club-styled satire for an audience of one in a living room in the middle of the afternoon, "I have a takeoff on the *Reader's Digest*—"

Tallulah interrupted, "When I was in the *Follies,* I had a number and I came down the stairs . . ." She proceeded to sing and act out the entire song.

"Now darling, tell me, what kind of comedy do you do? I don't want a vulgar comedian like David Burns. I want somebody young and clean and you look right, but I *have* to know what kind of stuff you do."

Once again, he tried, "Well, I have this takeoff on the *Reader's Digest*—"

"When I was in London," Tallulah started, and launched into another lengthy story.

The rest of the afternoon was the same: Mr. Kirkwood never got to do his prepared piece, he just listened to Tallulah.

At last, she sat down next to him on the sofa and said, "Well, darling, I just think you're perfect. You're funny, you're witty, I love what you do, and you look right. I'm going to have an entirely young cast, and I think you've got the part."

Suddenly she swung her legs up onto his lap, pulled the bottoms of her pants up, and said, "Have you ever seen more beautiful ankles than these, darling?"

If an experience like this ever comes your way, Great! But don't count on it happening more than once in your lifetime.

AUDITION ANNOUNCEMENTS: THE TRADE PAPERS

You can find out about auditions from notices that are posted in the weekly trade publications. *Variety* and *Backstage* are the two most widely read papers.

In New York City, *Variety* is usually published on Wednesdays and *Backstage* on Thursdays. Read these papers thoroughly, for they contain a wealth of information useful to anyone in the industry. *Backstage* has many more casting notices than *Variety,* and *Variety* has more general news of who's-doing-what in the various media—films, television, and recordings, as well as legitimate theatre.

What follows are some actual casting announcements culled from recent editions of these "trades":

PAPER MILL "LA CAGE"

8/11 & 8/12 at 10 AM-2 PM at Minskoff Rehearsal Studios, 1515 B'way., 3rd floor.
Paper Mill Playhouse, Millburn, New Jersey, will hold eligible performer chorus calls for "La Cage Aux Folles," at Minskoff Rehearsal Studio, 1515 Broadway, 3rd floor. COST contract. Angelo Del Rossi, exec. prod; Jim Pentacost, dir.; Kay Cameron, mus. dir.; Linda Haberman, choreo; Philip Wm. McKinley, casting dir. Rehearsals begin Aug. 25, runs from Sept. 14 thru Oct. 23. Chorus call procedures in effect. Special requirements for dancers: looking for strong dancers who sing well from all ethnic backgrounds to play the roles of the "Cagelles." Some roles require tapping but not all roles. Acrobatics and specialty dancing a plus but not required. Also need a male singer who has a very strong falsetto for the role of **Chantel**. Note: principal roles of **Francis** and **Anne** as well as the supporting roles may also be cast from this call. **Francis**: stage manager who is in love with Hannah, must be an excellent dancer and have a good comic acting ability; **Anne**: fiancee of Jean-Michel, must be an excellent dancer who is young and sincere. Also looking for the understudy for **Jacob**, the black butler/maid. Ineligible performers will be seen as time permits. Special Requirements for singers: Looking for all ethnic as well as character types for chorus roles. Performers must have excellent singing ability and be able to move well. Note: supporting roles will be cast from this call as well as understudies for some of the principal roles including **Jacob** and **Jean-Michel**. Ineligible performers will be seen as time permits. Paper Mill Playhouse encourages those of minority backgrounds to attend the call. Note that daytime rehearsals and performances are required. No phone calls to the theatre.
Thurs. Aug. 11—Eligible male dancers who sing, 10 AM
Thurs. Aug. 11—Eligible female dancers who sing, 2 PM
Fri. Aug. 12—Eligible male singers who move, 10 AM
Fri. Aug. 12—Eligible female singers who move, 1 PM

Off-Broadway

"And I Still Believe In Love" (M). Mini contract. Available parts: male, early 30s, baritone, handsome, struggling actor with tremendous promise and talent, lonely, driven, romantic; femme, early 30s, soprano, attractive, stylish corporate executive on the way up, been around, cynical, but still hopeful; male, early to mid-20s, baritone, tall, strong mid-western farm boy, very handsome in superb physical condition, non-macho masculine, sensitive, aggressive; femme, late 30s, early 40s, alto-mezzo, superb singer with exquisite face and figure. Successful cabaret singer, strong, vulnerable, very feminine and loving; male, early 20s, tenor, WASP upper-class collegiate type, handsome, in excellent physical condition, introspective, brooding, very masculine but sexually ambivalent; femme, black, early 20s, mezzo with good belt, social worker, alive and loving, stunningly beautiful, very innocent; male, late 20s-early 30s, tenor, bright, witty, cabaret pianist (playing skills helpful but not mandatory), strong comedic skills, handsome, charming, ready for anything; male, character actor, strong baritone and dancer to play 10 different roles, must be able to age from 25-65. Equity interviews being held Wednesday (29) and Thursday (1) from 9:30 a.m. to 1 p.m. and from 2-5:30 p.m., at the Actors Equity Audition Center (165 West 46th St., N.Y.). Non-Equity actors and actresses should send photos and resumes to BBS Productions, c/o Kojak (8 :\ West 5th St., N.Y. :3).

ATLANTIC CITY REVUE

8/2 at 3PM & 5PM at Minskoff Rehearsal Studio, 1515 B'way

Miller-Reich Enterprises will audition dancers for nightclub revue in the Showboat Hotel of Atlantic City. All-new production to replace the award-winning "Bodacious" by Sept. 1. Rehearsals in Atlantic City around Aug. 12. Must be extremely attractive and have strong dance background for very high-energy production. Auditions will be held on Tues. Aug. 2 at Minskoff Rehearsal Studios, 1515 B'way, as follows: Female dancers (min. 5'6")—3PM; Male dancers (min. 5'10")—5PM. Also seeking a male singer/dancer (experienced in both categories) for Atlantic City, as well as replacements for other Miller-Reich productions in Montreal, Baltimore & numerous cruise ships. Wear stage makeup at audition....ADVT.

B & T "ME & MY GIRL"

8/2 at 12 Noon at Marquis Theatre, use stage door on W. 45 St.

"There will be a call for eligible and non-eligible performers for the bus and truck company of "Me and My Girl" at the Marquis Theatre, use the stagedoor on W. 45 St., west of B'way. Bus & Truck contract. Male dancer/singer needed for immediate replacement. Eligible and non-eligible performers (eligible performers seen first). Looking for a strong tapper/jazz dancer with ballet background with tenor voice (needs to sustain an A). Must be 5'9" to 6'. Bring an up-tempo and a ballad and have jazz and tap shoes. Non-required call, no monitor required.

Tues. Aug. 2—Eligible, non-eligible males, 12 Noon.

Two of the blurbs contain cast breakdowns for the shows, which are prepared by the casting director along with the creative team. It indicates the ideal types of performers needed. Remember the discussion earlier of your type? Here's where you need to know it, so you can tell if anything in the breakdown sounds like a possible role for you. If so, follow the instructions in the announcement *to the letter.*

The breakdown notwithstanding, if the call is for a new show, it may be worth your while to attempt to get an audition even if you do not visualize yourself in one of the parts described. There's still a little leeway because, as I mentioned earlier, the show can change if the creative team gets excited about a particular performer. If it is an old show, or a current show seeking replacements—as in the above announcement for *La Cage aux Folles*—they'll stay fairly close to what was done in the past or to the types they are using now, even to the point of hiring clones.

Unfair as it may seem, often the only way you can get an audition scheduled for a principal role in a major Broadway production is through a reputable show-business agent. That's merely a fact of life, in the You-Can't-Fight-City-Hall Department. If you don't have an agent now, you will get one in time. In the meantime, there are plenty of auditions listed in the trade papers that you can attend at every stage of your career. See Appendix E for more information regarding agents and your career development.

NOW TO BEGIN . . .

I'm sure you have discerned from the foregoing that show business is tough, challenging, confusing, contradictory, intimidating—and more than a little discouraging. It's no secret that anyone who pursues a career in "The Biz" is in for a rough ride.

So think back to the beginning of this chapter and try to remember the exciting moment when you first decided to go into the business. Hold on to that moment and keep it somewhere in your memory. Feel lucky that you know what you want to do with your life and are in a position to pursue it. As Oscar Hammerstein II wrote in the song "Happy Talk" from *South Pacific:*

> You got to have a dream—
> If you don't have a dream
> How you gonna have a dream come true?

If you want a career in show business badly enough, you'll do whatever is necessary to make it happen. And the first step is learning how to master an audition.

PREPARATION—PART I: SELECTING

WHERE TO FIND AN ACCOMPANIST

One of the first things you will have to do is work with a pianist to help you find, prepare, and rehearse your material.

So where *do* you find an accompanist? Easy.

Anywhere.

Anyone who plays the piano is a potential accompanist. Yes, there is an art of sorts to accompanying; but for now, anyone will do—a friend, neighbor, voice teacher, or a relative are all good people to begin with. If they can't or won't play for you, ask if they know someone—you will undoubtedly find someone to work with through a recommendation.

Accompanists advertise in the trade papers and also post their business cards up on the bulletin boards at the rehearsal studios in New York City. Pick a few at random, call them up, and talk over the phone. Ask the price and where the sessions are held—in their home or in a studio. Find one you like talking to and arrange a session. No one can promise that the first time will work out for everyone, but if you don't like the person, find another quickly via the same means. At least now you'll have some basis for comparison.

As your credits grow and you get more accomplished, you will meet new people and thus be exposed to new musicians. Eventually, you'll be able to recognize the difference between good and bad pianists, and you will establish a rapport with certain musicians with whom you prefer to work.

But for starters, find anyone who seems suitable, and begin preparing.

YOUR AUDITION REPERTOIRE

You have to have something to do at an audition to show off your talent. Everyone is at the very least expected to have prepared two songs: a "ballad" and an "up-tune."

At its simplest, a ballad should show your emotional range and the way you phrase a lyric—your sensitivity to the words and thoughts.

An up-tune should show your sense of rhythm and how exciting you are as a performer. As a by-product, it can imply how enjoyable you would be to have in the cast. There are always so many problems attached to putting on a show that no one wants to work with people perceived as boring or unpleasant. So find a zingy up-number that shows off your sense of humor and sense of fun. Try to dazzle them.

The best kind of audition number in either category is a humorous one. The worst kind of number in either category is a song of self-pity. The latter type makes the listener uncomfortable, whereas the former allows the listener to sit back and relax. There is no rule anywhere that says you can't *entertain* at an audition. If you are able to unselfconsciously entertain the people casting a show, you may find yourself in the cast as a result.

In tandem, the ballad and the up-tune provide a needed

contrast for the listeners. And the two should be as different as possible in order to show the broadest range of your abilities. Find songs with which you connect emotionally and for which you are right agewise.

Emotional Considerations: Although your first choice for any song should of course be one you can sing believably without too much strain, you do not have to "agree" with all the lyrics of a song. If you have chosen an interesting song but the lyrics don't espouse your personal beliefs, you can still use it. Be someone else for those few minutes. Create a character to sing the song. Act.

Chronological Considerations: Anyone under the age of about forty, should not sing "Send In The Clowns" from *A Little Night Music* or "I'm Still Here" from *Follies* or "Before The Parade Passes By" from *Hello, Dolly!*. It is disorienting to see someone young, with no obvious backlog of experience, sing songs whose words were written to reflect the experiences of a mature person. The reverse is also true with songs like "I Feel Pretty" from *West Side Story* and "Tomorrow" from *Annie*. As you search for the songs to fill your portfolio, you will find there are dozens of candidates to choose from that will fit your age, range, and personality. Don't fret about not singing the few that don't.

BUILDING A SONG PORTFOLIO

Okay, ready for this one? I *know* that just two songs aren't enough. You must prepare more than two. If you spark interest from the director or one of the writers, they may need to see you show values other than the ones demonstrated in your ballad or up-tune, so it is advisable to prepare several different types of songs and to have them in performance-shape at all times. You should build a song portfolio. This will be a whole collection of songs you will use as audition material. In this portfolio you should have at least one of each of the following types of songs:

1. Ballad

2. Up-tune

3. Comedy song

4. Contemporary (rock) song

5. Patter song

6. Standard torch song—only for women

At almost every audition I have ever played, someone sitting behind the decision-table has asked to hear a song from most of these categories. Too many times performers have only two songs prepared—sometimes only one—and when asked for additional material, instead of saying, "No, I haven't prepared anything else," they try to improvise something with the pianist. Instead of impressing the production team with their versatility, they generally make a mess of their audition. It's better to be prepared.

The very notion of having to sing a comedy song throws performers and coaches alike into such a tizzy—as if they had never even heard of the concept before. This is probably because good comedy songs are notoriously difficult to find. The same songs tend to be used over and over. The works of Noel Coward, Howard Dietz, E. Y. Harburg, Lorenz Hart, and Cole Porter—to mention just a few of the immortals—are chock full of great, little-known, sure-fire comic material. Finding these songs takes a lot of digging, but they are there to be found.

Always keep in mind that the people auditioning you are usually frighteningly well-versed in the standard musical theatre song repertoire. This means that it will be a virtually impossible task to find a comedy song that your judges can't recite along with you. Do not let this fact intimidate you—just do not expect laughs where the laughs should be, and do not under any circumstances attempt to perform all the extant verses of the song you select. Just once through the main melody will be sufficient to demonstrate your way with comic material.

At a recent audition, all the actors were asked to prepare a comedy song. One young man entered the room and said, "I don't have a comedy song so I'll just sing 'Being Alive' very fast and see if it's funny."

It wasn't.

Here's a dangerous idea that can work: Take a standard song that everyone knows and is sick of and rewrite the lyrics a la some of Allan Sherman's material. Be careful—your rewrite must be very clever and you must never do it in front of the original writers.

As for the contemporary number, please pick one with a pretty, singable melody. Although the theme song from the motion picture *Shaft* may have won the Academy Award as best song of its year, it hardly has a catchy lyric. Turn instead to something soft-rock, such as songs by Neil Diamond, Dan Fogelberg, Billy Joel, Melissa Manchester, Randy Newman, Paul Simon, or Stevie Wonder.

A "patter song" is one that has a complicated, wordy lyric. There's at least one in every Gilbert and Sullivan operetta—and any of them will suffice. Cole Porter, Noel Coward, and Lorenz Hart each wrote many of them. Another recent example is "Another Hundred People" from *Company*—although, as I will discuss later, you would be wise to avoid Stephen Sondheim's songs.

Torch songs: Prime examples would be "The Man That Got Away," from the movie *A Star Is Born,* by Harold Arlen and Ira Gershwin; "The Man I Love," by the Gershwin brothers— George and Ira—; and "Bill," from *Show Boat,* by Jerome Kern and P.G. Wodehouse. Linda Ronstadt recorded 32 suitable torch/ballads for her albums "What's New" and "Lush Life," and "For Sentimental Reasons." Check your Judy Garland and Barbra Streisand records for some choice, little-known ones.

You may want to add a Country-Western song to the above list. Although it is rarely called for, it couldn't hurt to have one ready.

Steel yourself—here's another zinger:

You should also have a back-up song ready for each of the categories.

Why?

Because what if the person just ahead of you—and this happens all the time!—sings the same song you were planning to do. Now don't say, "But that happened to me and I know I sang the song a hundred times better than the one who did it before me." That may indeed be true, but please understand the point of view of the people listening. They don't want to be bored by hearing the identical song twice in a row. That's why you have—and should use—your back-up song.

I once played the auditions for a touring company of *The Wiz.* Eighteen people in a row—I counted—sang either "God Bless The Child" or "Be A Lion," and not one person brought another song to even offer a choice. It drove the director and the choreographer mad because after a short while the actors lost their individuality, and it was difficult afterwards to remember accurately who sang better than who.

If you have talent, your alternate choice will show it off just as well as your first choice. After all, didn't you choose both on the basis of their ability to do just that?

People are always uncertain about how long their songs should be. The quick answer: Probably no more than two minutes for each song. The people auditioning you make an immediate judgment based on your look as soon as you enter the room. They are also extremely practiced listeners and can tell rather quickly whether or not you have the requisite vocal ability; some musical directors boast that they know within the first eight bars of a song. So doing a long song with many choruses is rather an imposition, no matter how good you are. You can make a clear case for your talent in a very short time. If your song goes on for too long, there is a great possibility that you will be cut off midstream. I promise you, you'll feel terrible if this happens.

Remember the expression, leave them wanting more? If you doubt the wisdom of this, take a look at the W.C. Fields movie *The Old Fashioned Way*. In it, Fields is forced to hear Cleopatra Pepperday—an untalented, wealthy woman—audition for him. He wants her money to put on a creaky melodrama in her town. She wants to be in the show, so in her living room he listens to her sing "The Seashell Song." At the end of the first chorus, Fields politely rises from his seat, applauds, and starts to heartily and insincerely congratulate her as if it were the end of the song, only to have her launch into the next verse. This continues a few more times. Mr. Fields's hilarious facial expressions and antics are representative of what the casting team goes through when you sing long songs.

Use two minutes as your guide. If your favorite song takes considerably longer than that to make a complete statement lyrically, *choose another song*.

WHAT NOT TO SING

The opinions that follow are admittedly debatable, but they do come from experience. Sometimes I feel that singers resist the advice in this section merely because it means they have to do some homework—once I have eliminated 99 percent of the songs they know as potential audition material, they are left with a lot of hard work in front of them, finding and selecting what are considered to be better choices.

There are certain kinds of songs that don't do for you the wonders you think they will if you sing them. Heading this category is anything extremely well-known. As I mentioned before, the people auditioning you more often than not can sing along with any of the familiar songs from Broadway shows, even from the unsuccessful ones. They like those songs. They may even *love* some of those songs. But hearing them in an audition situation is, frankly, boring. The purpose of an audition is to make the director pay close attention to you and give you serious consideration. Well, one way to accomplish this from your point of view is to sing something the director doesn't know by heart.

One woman protested, "But I thought people liked to hear familiar songs?" Yes, they do, but not at an audition. You must perk them up—in a sense, *force* them to listen closely. You cannot accomplish that if you lull them with the familiarity of your material.

So at the center of my arguments about auditions is the theory that you should sing well-crafted material which is not well-known; actually, the more obscure the better.

However, there seems to be an exception to this. I recently played auditions for a Country-Western show and it was greatly appreciated when someone came in with a Country-Western standard rather than an obscure song in the genre. The difference in quality between the Nashville hits and the misses is significant, so if you are auditioning for that kind of show and you can't find a dynamite unknown song, don't look too hard. Stick with a well-known one that has a great, singable melody and actable lyrics.

Don't sing songs closely associated with a particular singer—"signature" songs. If, for example, you sing "Over The Rainbow," the listeners will unconsciously and involuntarily compare you with Judy Garland—no matter how good you are, you can't make people forget the original rendition. You want *your* talent evaluated and, hopefully, appreciated. You don't want your valuable audition time spent standing in someone else's shadow.

I'll never forget the young man who sang the Barbra Streisand slowed-down version of "Happy Days Are Here Again," complete with Streisand-like arm gestures. He was genuinely surprised and a little miffed when, after he sang, the director suggested the man sing something on his own and not flagrantly copy someone else's style.

At one audition a few years ago, a young lady sang "Nothing" from *A Chorus Line*. After the song, the director took her aside and explained that because she did a song that was from a show currently running on Broadway, it was very difficult to evaluate her particular gifts. He went on to say that the song wasn't a particularly good choice because the exquisite performance by the original actress, Priscilla Lopez, was so ingrained in his memory and in the memories of the others looking at this girl that they couldn't get a clear sense of what she could really do. He advised her to prepare another song and come to the callback. Tears began to well up in her eyes. She said, "My mother told me I do this song *better* than Priscilla Lopez."

In Appendix A you will find a long list of the songs that are, at the time of this writing, considered to be the most overdone audition songs, and should therefore be avoided. In 1988. Obviously, as tastes and times change, so will this list. Be on your guard. When in doubt, ask questions.

Try to put yourself in your listener's place when you select your material. Remember that depending on the time of your audition, they either have a long day ahead of or behind them. Taking this into consideration, stay away from songs that are spiritually or morally uplifting—"You'll Never Walk Alone"; relentlessly cheerful—"On A Wonderful Day Like Today"; or so cloyingly sweet as to send the listeners instantly into a diabetic coma—of which there are numerous examples, many written by my idols, the Messrs. Rodgers and Hammerstein. Also be aware that songs of self-aggrandizement provoke perverse thoughts in the listener. Examples:

"I'm The Greatest Star"—*According to whom?*

"You're Gonna Hear From Me"—*Not if I have anything to say about it!*

"I've Gotta Be Me"—*But why?*

"Nothing Can Stop Me Now"—*Oh, yeah? I can!*

It's usually not a great idea to sing original songs—either

written by yourself, by your pianist, or by your friends—at auditions. These songs are not always as good as you think they are. Being fair about this, obscure show songs are often obscure for very good reasons as well. But if you've made a poor choice, and the song you're performing makes the mice put in earplugs, and someone in the room asks, "*Where* did you find *that* song," you're much better off being able to say, "It was cut from *Via Galactica*," rather than saying that it was written by a friend. There are exceptions to this, of course, just as there are exceptions to all the points in this book. But bear in mind that directors have rejected many a performer because of a bad song choice. Why risk it?

Don't kill yourself at an audition. I feel like I'm divulging a well-kept secret when I tell you it's not necessary to perform a difficult or tricky song to be noticed. That type of number usually contains many pitfalls and traps that you could easily fall into if you are edgy. For a time, the song "What Are You Doing The Rest Of Your Life?" was a popular audition number. It's a stunning song, but it has a melodic line composed of small, chromatic intervals that are hard to sing accurately in the best of circumstances. Over the years many good singers have inadvertently gone off-pitch singing that song. The moral is: Sing something simple. Sing a song that won't work against you if you're nervous.

Unless it is specifically requested in advance, do not sing songs written by the composer or authors you are auditioning for. The same goes for songs from shows with which the director, choreographer, or musical director were closely associated. This point was strongly echoed by everyone I spoke to while preparing this book. If you think they will be flattered by your choices you are right, but since most—if not all—composers and lyricists have very definite ideas about how their songs should be performed, they will be busy *comparing* during your audition, rather than watching and listening.

And if you think they will be impressed with your "different," "novel," or "definitive" rendition of their material, you may be correct—but not under these circumstances. You are there to show off yourself and your talent to best advantage. You don't want to waste your precious few minutes of audition time distracting your listeners. If they are for any reason whatsoever displeased with your performance of their material, you will have wasted all your preparation and may as well kiss that job good-bye.

However, when you audition as a replacement in a production that is running or for a touring company of an established show you are often asked to prepare a song from the show and sing that as your audition piece. Taking this request a step further, the *Les Miserables* production staff asked everyone auditioning for the Los Angeles and Canadian production to not only prepare a specific song from the score but to imitate the performance on the cast album as closely as possible. When the production staff wants you to do this they will make their wishes known through the casting director. If you do not get a specific request, do not sing songs from the show.

A WORD ON SONDHEIM . . .

Stephen Sondheim, one of the theatre's true geniuses, has written the music and lyrics for many brilliant, melodic, witty, singable, and highly actable songs. His material is challenging, complex, and rewarding to perform—not only because he understands the capabilities and limitations of voices, but also because he has a thorough knowledge of the theatre and the possibilities for songs within the framework of a show. Mr. Sondheim conceives his songs as complete one-act plays, with a beginning, a middle, and an end. Many of his songs can stand alone, outside the context of the show, and would therefore seem to make very good audition pieces.

Now for the bad news.

Most people think it inadvisable to sing Mr. Sondheim's songs at auditions.

Quite frankly, his songs are so good they can magnify any flaws in your voice or technique. Remember that the purpose of the audition is to show off yourself at your *best*. And if you are nervous, or have had a particularly busy day prior to the audition, or are not thoroughly warmed up, his songs will not serve you well.

Also, the same rule about the people who audition you knowing the songs too well applies doubly here. There are so many songs to pick and choose from that will be better for you during an audition situation than any of Mr. Sondheim's—save his splendid material for your club act.

WHERE TO FIND SONGS

I can't print a list of the songs I feel would be appropriate for auditions. As you will see, there are so many possibilities that I would be severely limiting you by even listing a hundred or so. What I can do is tell you where *you* can find good material. It's not that difficult to do—it just takes time. And considerable research. But trust me, the results will pay off a thousand-fold over the years.

Too many performers know very little about the musical theatre. I can't think of any other occupation where its practitioners are not required to have even a minimal knowledge of their field. Can you imagine a doctor, lawyer, architect, or engineer doing his work without thoroughly knowing the history and craft of his chosen profession, and instead operating on "feelings," "gut instincts," and "natural abilities"?

When I was growing up and developing my interest in theatre, I read Stanley Green's wonderful book, *The World of Musical Comedy,* cover to cover. Many times. It's still an excellent book, still in print (New York: Da Capo Press, fourth edition, 1984), and I still refer to it from time to time. If you seek this book out and read it, it will give you, in a highly entertaining way, an overview of where the musical theatre of today has come from.

Ditto another, more recent book, Lehman Engel's *The American Musical Theatre* (New York: Collier Books, a division of Macmillan Publishing Co., 1975).

In addition, I believe that every aspiring performer should have a basic knowledge of and familiarity with the songs in all the major musicals that have been performed on Broadway. You can call this part of your training, Doing Your Homework.

The minimum list of shows you should know includes the following:

The five mega-hit shows by Rodgers and Hammerstein— *Oklahoma!, Carousel, South Pacific, The King and I,* and *The Sound of Music;*

Lerner and Loewe's *Brigadoon, My Fair Lady,* and *Camelot;*

Jerry Herman's *Hello, Dolly!, Mame* and *La Cage aux Folles;*

Andrew Lloyd Webber's phenomenal successes: *Evita, Cats,* and *The Phantom of the Opera;*

Stephen Sondheim's *Company, Follies, A Little Night Music,* and *Sweeney Todd;*

Along with the following—*A Chorus Line, Annie Get Your Gun, Bells Are Ringing, Cabaret, Damn Yankees, Fiddler on the Roof, Finian's Rainbow, Funny Girl, Guys and Dolls, Gypsy, Kismet, Kiss Me Kate, Les Miserables, Man of la Mancha, Me and My Girl, The Fantasticks, The Music Man, The Pajama Game,* and *West Side Story.*

This is by no means an exhaustive list, but if at the very least you know these shows, you will have a pretty solid grounding in what a good theatre song is, so when you select your songs you will have a strong basis for comparison. As a by-product, you will have a large list of songs *not* to sing—ever—at an audition.

Why?

Because the songs in all the above shows are much too well known—go back to "What Not To Sing" for the explanation. But many's the time a director has said to a singer something like, "Do you have anything similar to 'It Only Takes a Moment' from *Hello, Dolly!*"—and the singer has sheepishly admitted not knowing "It Only Takes a Moment." Knowing these shows gives you not only a background in your chosen field, but also a common vocabulary with your peers.

Also, the roster of musicals performed in summer stock and dinner theatres across the country is largely culled from the above list, augmented by whatever fairly recent shows have just become available. When those theatres put out audition announcements in the trades, they only list the names of the shows, not full cast breakdowns. If you know the shows, you automatically know which roles are right for you.

Okay, now that you have taken the time to do the above, where do you find those "obscure" songs that promise to work miracles for you?

The answer is coming in just a moment.

Be aware of this: There have been well over 1,000 musicals performed on and off Broadway since the beginning of this century. Each show contains, on an average, 12 to 14 songs. Doing some simple multiplication in round numbers, we're now in the range of about 12,000 songs. Add to this number several hundred film musicals with about 5 or 6 songs in each movie and our total is now well over 13,500. To this total we can, if we wish, add songs that were written strictly for the pop market—or Tin Pan Alley as it was called in an earlier age—and the numbers skyrocket.

I do hear your immediate protests: "Most of those songs aren't that good, or they're not usable for our purposes. After all, your total includes opening choruses and other discountable material."

Fine, I say. Throw out three-fourths of them and we still have a staggering number to select from.

So, if there are so many, why do people pick the same few over and over? Because, admittedly, many—if not most—of the songs I am alluding to are out-of-print, unpublished, or similarly unavailable for perusal, therefore leaving the readily available standard repertoire to choose from. Which is what most people do.

We happen to be living in a lucky era right now. For finding songs, that is. There have been revues upon revues in the last few years, presenting well-known and not-so-well-known songs by both major and—pardon the easy categorizing—minor theatre composers. If you didn't see any of them, perhaps you know someone who was in one who may have the music and could recommend some songs.

Also, Ben Bagley's Painted Smiles Record Company* has by now issued more than forty albums devoted to the undeservedly lesser-known songs of nearly every famous Broadway songwriter. The records, which are widely available in many record stores— and by mail, directly from the company—are a treasure-trove of great audition material.

There is also a company called Music Masters*, which at the time of this writing has issued over sixty albums containing both previously out-of-print recordings and never-before-issued-on-record material by show and movie composers and lyricists. Their "Music of Broadway" series alone—eighteen discs full of fabu-

---

* See Appendix G for addresses and telephone numbers.

lous songs—will provide you with dozens of choices for audition songs.

You should also check out early Frank Sinatra, Dean Martin, and Peggy Lee albums. These singers had great songwriters penning their material, and you just may find a not-too-well-known song to your liking among them. Obviously there are many more singers to add to the three mentioned—look through and listen to the records in your parents' collection.

So, now you've found a song you like and you don't have any sheet music. What do you do?

First, you call whichever local store sells sheet music to see if, by chance, they have it—most stores in small neighborhoods have very small selections, though. Check with your musical friends. Look in the piano bench in your parents' home. Ask your piano-playing aunt who, if she had the song, would be delighted to give it to you. I asked her.

If you've still yielded no results, don't be discouraged. The great search is on! Your next step is to call a store like Colony* in New York City, which maintains one of the largest collections— for sale, of course—of in-print sheet music. See if the song is still available. Aside from individual song sheets, the song may be published in one of the hundreds of published collections— including so-called *Fake Books,* which provide lead vocal lines and chord symbols for about 1,000 songs per book; as well as specialized volumes with generic titles on the order of *Great Songs of the 1960's.* Several decades worth of these last were issued.

If you have no luck at Colony, or a similar store, call the Music Exchange*, also in New York City, which sells its extensive collection of out-of-print music.

* See Appendix G for addresses and telephone numbers.

If you are still coming a cropper, go to the Library and Museum of the Performing Arts at Lincoln Center. On the first floor, in the music division, there exists a large and unusual collection of out-of-print sheet music, which can be photocopied on the premises for fifteen cents a page. There is an index of songs by title only, so be sure you know the correct title.

If you still haven't found the song through any of the aforementioned sources and if the sales help at the stores or the librarians can't recommend anywhere else to try, you can surely get a pianist to write out the music—at least a lead sheet—taking it off the record on which you found it.

The above suggestions certainly do not represent the only places to find songs. I offer them merely as a starting point, and I hope my thoughts will inspire and trigger some clever ones of your own. Undoubtedly the pianist with whom you work will have some ideas for you; but please, do not rely on his advice alone without doing some work on your own.

No, it's not easy, but doing all that listening and research can only help you in the long run. After all, you are immersing yourself in the worlds of theatre and music—could there be more pleasurable homework?

PREPARATION — PART II: THE MECHANICS

HOW TO PREPARE YOUR MUSIC

Here's the only irrefutable rule of auditioning:

If you are auditioning for a musical, you must always bring your own music.

I can't stress this strongly enough. Once upon a time, I accompanied someone on his audition for the original cast of *Barnum*. There were about thirty-five guys seated in the first few rows of the Edison Theatre, where the auditions were being held. The first man was called. He stepped onto the stage, conferred with the pianist, then went over to center stage and sang, "Happy Birthday."

"You didn't bring any music with you?" asked Joe Layton, the director.

"No," replied the actor.

The second guy was called, and surprisingly the exact same process was repeated.

Mr. Layton stood up and said, "How many of you don't have your own music?"

More than half of those present raised their hands.

So Mr. Layton had to make his choices after hearing about twenty actors in a row sing "Happy Birthday."

Okay. Let's keep things in perspective. That's not such a terrible anecdote. The world didn't come to an end. Mr. Layton didn't run out of the Edison Theatre screaming and immediately quit the business. *Barnum* wasn't cancelled or postponed until those auditioning could get their act together.

And as far as I was concerned, this story had a happy ending: My friend—who did *not* sing "Happy Birthday" but, rather, sang an obscure song we prepared and rehearsed—was chosen for the show and played in it throughout its New York run.

But I would bet a substantial sum of money that had all the auditioners prepared songs, a slightly different group of them would have made telephone calls to their families saying they were cast in a show.

More perspective now.

The above occurrence was a rarity. Most people who audition for musical shows know they should prepare a song and bring the music. Although the number of unenlightened performers makes the previous case noteworthy, it was not an isolated happening. I have sat at the piano during many other auditions at which at least one person came up to the piano stating, "I didn't know I had to bring music."

Always carry music with you, especially if you're not sure.

But if you come to an audition and don't have music, *don't ever sing a cappella*. It is extraordinarily difficult to stay on pitch without the aid of a musical instrument and it is extremely awkward-sounding. There has never been a reason good enough to warrant it. If your music is, for whatever reason, unavailable, it is best to attempt to reschedule your audition to a time when you can bring the music. If you insist on singing a cappella, the only thing you will accomplish is writing off the audition. You might as well stay home.

On the other side of the coin, there is an astounding number of talented performers who come to auditions smartly dressed, every hair in place, in all visible ways charming and gracious—the very model of perfection. And, yes, they even have music with them. But the music they hand to the pianist is distressingly illegible. The only thing I can attribute this to is perhaps an unconscious feeling on the actor's part that his music is no more than a necessary evil. Since many actors do not read music, I would further assume they really can't tell if their music is truly playable or not.

Accompanists often wonder why, with the inexpensive cost and relative availability of duplicating services, so much music carried to auditions is in large books, or if a single copy, it is usually unattached, in an advanced state of deterioration. Some people are even aware of their music's condition. They apologize, saying, "I know I should get another copy of this song—I'm sorry it's in such bad shape." Or they offer an excuse, such as, "I didn't have time to tape the music together."

Enough complaining—here comes the advice.

First and foremost, your music must be legible. If it isn't, you cannot expect anyone to be able to play it.

Next, keep in mind two facts about the pianist provided by the production company:

1. He already *has* his job; don't make him audition his skills by making him fight his way through an unplayable copy of your song.

2. The pianist—all rumors to the contrary—is there to work for you; and he will, if provided the basic professional courtesies. Like having your music properly prepared.

TRANSPOSITION

If you are singing a song that has been published, and you have the sheet music, and you do it in the published key, you are indeed fortunate. If you aren't so lucky, you will have to have your music specially prepared or doctored—transposed—to make it functional.

Songs that are published are usually issued in a key deemed either by the composer or someone at the publisher's office to be the easiest for a mass audience to deal with—even if it is different from the key the song was originally written or performed in. For example, in the show *Funny Girl,* Barbra Streisand sang the song "People" in the key of A-flat. The sheet music was transposed up to the key of B-flat, even though that put the song out of the range of a lot of singers. This was done because B-flat is considered to be an easier key than A-flat for amateur pianists. So if you've ever sung along comfortably with a recording, then purchased the sheet music and couldn't reach the high notes when they were played on the piano, now you know why.

Every song can either be transposed up or down. With your accompanist or vocal coach try several different keys until you find the one that sounds and feels comfortable for your voice.

Many times people have walked over to the piano at an audition, handed their music to a pianist they were seeing for the first time and said, "Can you play this in a key I can sing it in?" What does the singer expect—that the pianist is Marvo the Magnificent Mind Reader? How could the pianist possibly know the singer's voice and which key would be suitable? Equally bad are those who say, for example, "Play 'As Time Goes By' in D-flat." I do agree that any pianist worth his salt should know any standard song like "As Time Goes By," and should be able to play it off the top of his head in most keys—but why leave anything to chance? Bring a copy of the music that has been prepared in advance—*in your key*—so the pianist can be comfortable playing for you, thus giving you the support you need and deserve.

If your music is to be transposed, it is advisable to have it fully written out in your key. However, this can be expensive, depending on the arrangement and number of pages; so it is permissible and quite common—but mind you, not as good as having the music fully written out—to have the transposed chords written over the measures. Keep the original chords visible— don't scratch them out or use white-out—and have the transposed chords written in a different-color ink, usually red. That makes it easier for pianists to follow and play from.

Please remember that in preparing music that must be transposed, writing the new chords over the measures is the barest minimum you should have done. As I said before, never come in with the music in the original key and say, "Play it in C-sharp." It only takes ten to fifteen minutes at the most for a musician to write in the proper chords. Don't ever say there wasn't time to have it done.

Also—do not under any circumstances present music on which the original chords plus *two* sets of transposed chords are visible. Since it is for your own personal use and not for sale, the original music can be copied as many times as you like, and you can have each copy transposed once to a different key.

PROFESSIONAL COPYING

There are professional copyists who do beautiful work hand-copying music in ink. It may be worth it to you to have your music meticulously prepared, especially if the music is transposed, or if you are using a complicated or special arrangement. Some copyists put their business cards, with their phone numbers, on the bulletin boards at the audition studios, and some

advertise in the trades; so if you don't have any personal refer-
ences—ask your friends first—contact one, and if he's unknown
to you, ask to see samples of his work before you give your song
to be worked on.

Standard minimum fees for this kind of work—according to
Local 802 of the American Federation of Musicians in New
York—run $9.44 per page, which includes the vocal line, the
piano part, and the lyrics. If the music is to be transposed, it will
cost an additional 50 percent per page, bringing the total to
exactly $14.16 per page. These prices are current as of September
1988. Unions being what they are, the prices go up every year or
two. Also, fees vary slightly with the union locals across the
country. I quote prices here merely to give you an approximate
idea of the cost.

If your music is hand-copied, the lyrics and the melody line
must be fully written out on the music. So-called charts—a sheet
of music divided into the number of bars in the song with only
the chord changes indicated—may be sufficient for jazz musicians
and for your own accompanist, but they are almost useless for
anyone else. It takes the same ten to fifteen minutes at most to
write down the lyrics on a chart. Why it is not done universally is
beyond me. There is one major reason for having both the lyrics
and the melody on the music page: If you forget the words or go
off-pitch for any reason, the pianist can come to your rescue.

THE CARE AND FEEDING OF YOUR MUSIC

Most of the pianos we pianists find to play on in audition
rooms are, to put it nicely, not in the best of shape. Often there
are several keys broken, and rarely are they in perfect tune.

Another almost standard feature of those instruments is the
lack of a proper stand for sheet music. Which is why a lot of the

highly original ways people have of putting their music together simply don't work. It may be the piano's fault and not the actor's, but whatever the reason, it's mighty hard to play well for somebody when the music won't stay upright, or when it falls off the stand onto the keys, onto the pianist's lap, or onto the floor. And it *does* fall—with amazing regularity.

Sheet music you purchase from stores is printed on fairly sturdy paper—sturdier, anyway, than stationery or conventional bond paper. If you are going to use a photocopy of your music at an audition, it is better to have it copied onto a heavyweight stock—your music will stay in acceptable shape a lot longer. Remember, the music isn't staying at home, lying on your piano. It is being transported constantly, shoved in your dance bag or briefcase, and touched and played by many different hands. Regular paper wasn't designed to take that kind of abuse. Some neighborhood copy centers routinely have what is sometimes referred to as card-stock on hand. Otherwise, you can take your music to one of several places that service the music industry. The names, addresses, and phone numbers of a few of these places are listed in Appendix G, at the back of this book. The cost of photocopying onto this kind of paper usually runs around forty to fifty cents a page.

Please do not, for any reason whatsoever, fold your music in half. It just won't stay put even on a good music stand if it has been folded. Keep it flat.

Some people—especially some voice teachers—advocate placing each page of music between sheets of transparent plastic in a loose-leaf notebook. Certainly this presents a neat appearance, but there are several problems. The book is simply too cumbersome and heavy to carry around. The plastic covers tend to reflect light. Because it is impossible to control the light source in an audition room, your music may be hard to read from. In addition, the plastic pages are hard to grasp. Pianists often inadvertently turn two pages at a time. Or the plastic sticks to the binder rings and the pages can't be turned at all.

Individual copies of your songs are a much better solution.

Keep your audition songs in one place. Get a strong folder or envelope to store them in—it should be sturdy enough to travel with. Do not put extraneous music in the portfolio, and do not remove any of the songs from the portfolio lest they not be there when you need them.

To be on the safe side, you should have a spare copy of your music tucked away at home. What if you lose your bag? What if you leave your music on the piano at the audition and can't remember later where it is? My personal collection of music grew significantly in this manner. Consider this a word to the wise. Or is it "a stitch in time"?

So now that you have your music copied, the pages must be attached.

Never staple your music together. It is impossible to play from.

Always tape your music. There are a lot of reasons why you shouldn't leave your sheet music unattached; I mentioned earlier about pages falling to the floor—so all I'll add here is that I wish I had a dollar for every person who handed me their sheets of unattached music with a page missing, usually the last. "Oh, gosh, I'm sorry," they say, "I must have left that page at home." An all-too-obviously avoidable situation. (See Appendix C for directions on the most effective way of taping your music together.)

The first time playing through any piece of music there is one problem for every pianist: page turns. The pianist, all rumors to the contrary, is human, with only two hands. It is mighty difficult to turn a page of music while at the same time keeping the rhythm and the accompaniment going of a song he may not be overly familiar with. If your music is not the standard store-bought version, make sure it is printed on only one side of the page and accordion-folded as described in Appendix C. This way, the music can be opened up flat and there will be no page turns to worry about. Four to five pages across will fit on most pianos. If your music is longer than five pages, your song is too long.

INTERPRETATION: ACTING THE SONG

This book will not go into the techniques of vocal production. That subject could fill a volume of its own. So what this part covers is not how to sing a song, but rather a very brief discussion of how to perform a song.

In the words of casting director and former theatrical agent Jeffrey Dunn, "Singing is acting on pitch." (See Appendix E for an interview with Mr. Dunn.)

To elaborate, it's not enough to merely learn the words and the notes. You must completely understand what the song is saying and figure out how to communicate its meaning.

Take a look at the structure of the song. Is there a "verse"—a section which precedes the main melody? Verses are written to set up the song's subject matter. Often the main body of a song—the chorus—is written in general terms—a bid for wide-spread appeal. But the verse makes the song specific to a certain situation and can delineate a character. While verses are important lyrically, they are usually very simple and unmemorable musically. An almost singular exception to this is the haunting verse to Jerome Kern and Oscar Hammerstein's "All The Things You Are." But because of the general rule, verses are almost always performed "freely," that is, not in tempo, with maximum attention given to the words. Underneath this, the pianist usually plays a minimal accompaniment, following the singer's lead.

So now that you know the song's structure, continue your analysis by clearly defining the character who is singing the song. Ask yourself, What is he or she trying to accomplish by singing? What is the subtext? Subtext is the thoughts *behind* the words— sometimes very different from what is actually being sung.

After you answer these questions for yourself, speak the lyric out loud as if it were a monologue. Do this a few times. Rephrase the song in your own words. Then sing it again to the music—but this time sing the lyric as simply as if you were speaking it.

To continue your analysis of the song, find the natural phrases of the lyric and see how they rise or fall with the music. If you train yourself to think of the song as a series of phrases, rather than as a sequence of individual words, your performance will be more natural. I always advise people to sing the *lyric,* and not to be concerned with making pretty sounds at the expense of the meaning or intent of the song.

Never distort the English language as you sing. Good song-writers are extremely careful to accent the correct syllables. If the song you have chosen seems to force the language in places, you can usually bend the words back into their natural sound and compensate for the unevenness when you perform. Look for the rhymes and make sure you rhyme them properly as you sing.

A question I get asked a lot is, "Where should I breathe?" There is a simple, all-purpose, all-inclusive answer to that: Always breathe with the lyric. Breathe when there is a pause in the thought. Look for punctuation marks, chiefly the commas and the periods. You can always take a breath wherever there is a period and, depending on the speed of the music, usually where there is a comma. And if you sometimes have to take a big breath and make it last a long time, it is probably unavoidable. The result of all this intellectualization of the breathing process is that your interpretation should sound intelligent.

Following my earlier suggestions about listening to recordings, try to listen to more than one singer perform your song. It's not always possible, especially with obscure songs, but you'll be amazed at the different ways a song can be interpreted. As an exercise, listen to Stephen Sondheim's magnificent song "Send In The Clowns," from *A Little Night Music,* as performed by Glynis Johns on the original Broadway cast recording; by Jean Simmons on the original London cast recording; by Elizabeth Taylor on the movie soundtrack; and in the pop field, by Frank Sinatra and Judy Collins. Each sings the same song in fairly similar arrangements, but there are worlds of difference in the nuances that these very talented performers find in the identical material, without distorting the song's meaning.

Some of the music put in front of me at the piano has been heavily annotated with acting suggestions, such as "Open up here," "Think of all people in this situation," "Look serious," and "Arms up." Although gestures can be expressive and effective, don't overdo them. They must be derived naturally. Nor while singing should you ever illustrate the various words or images in the song with your hands, as if performing for the hearing-impaired. Try to think in terms of the complete thought or the intent. If there is a particular word that conjures up a strong image, use it to your advantage, but first understand what mood and effect the *entire* song is going after.

It would be wonderful if you could move and sing at the same time. Standing like a statue won't do. Find some movement that is natural, loose, and appropriate for the song you're singing. If you have a tendency towards stiffness—as in, "He is so wooden, if you light a match to him, he'll go up in flames"—get a friend who directs and/or choreographs to help devise some easy and effective movement for you. It could make all the difference. Do not do something choreographed either by your singing teacher or by your mother unless your mother is Agnes de Mille; it is sure to look amateurish. And, if you are working with a director or choreographer on your audition, do not, during a singing audition, do a heavily choreographed song and dance number. If you begin something which looks too intricate, someone from the production team will probably say, "Don't move. Just sing." If the people sitting behind the desk want to see how well you dance they will set up a specific dance audition at a separate time, where you will have to learn and perform specially prepared movements supervised by the show's choreographer or dance captain.

To sum up: Singing is merely a form of communication. Think of a song as a sung monologue. Acting (and moving) while singing is not as difficult as you may think it is if you aren't tense and up-tight about it. If you understand what it is you want to communicate, you will find that the meaning, the breathing, and the movement will all fall into place naturally.

WORKING WITH A VOCAL COACH

Don't confuse a vocal coach with a singing teacher. A singing teacher can help you with the actual production of sound and with breathing and support, and can also give lots of other technical advice. If you have vocal problems, or merely need advice on how to sing better, go to a singing teacher rather than a coach.

The vocal coach is used for other services, mainly for guiding you in putting over the song to maximum effectiveness. At some point you will have to work with one to rehearse your material. Often, but not always, your accompanist is also a vocal coach. Since anyone who plays the piano can call himself a vocal coach, there are several things to keep in mind so as to get the most for your money.

You should work with a coach who is also a pianist.

Your coach must be able to help you determine whether the music needs to be transposed and must have the skill to actually play the transposition. Then, he should be able to prepare your music so that anyone else can play it easily—at the very least your vocal coach should be able to accurately write the new chords in on your music. Be aware that some music you purchase may have inaccurate chords printed—your pianist should be able to spot and correct the errors, so that when it is transposed, the chords are correct.

As I said before—and it bears repeating—it only takes ten to fifteen minutes at the most to write new chords on an existing song, so there's never any reason to say that there wasn't time to get the song transposed. Lots of people use this excuse!

Know the key you are performing in. It makes you sound smart and knowledgeable to be able to say, "I do the song in the key of C and the music is in the correct key" or, "I'm doing this in E-flat, and the transposed chords are written in red ink"— instead of having to say, "I don't know what key I do this in. Isn't it on the music?" You don't even have to know what C or E-flat means. The pianist at the audition will know and you both will be more secure.

Another true story: At one audition an actor gave me his music and, without saying a word, headed for the center of the room. I called him back. "What kind of introduction would you like?" I asked. "I don't know," he said, "what kinds of introductions are there?"

The real answer to that question is there are many different kinds. From simple bell tones to arpeggiated chords to full four- or eight-measure piano solos. With your vocal coach, pick a simple, functional intro that will help you establish both the key and the mood for the beginning of the song. And get it written down so that any person playing your music will play the same thing. A common complaint I hear from singers is, "I had no idea *what* the pianist was playing for an intro. I couldn't find my first note." This is easily avoidable if the introduction is notated.

Not only the introduction, but the ending, as well as cuts or repeats should be clearly marked and indicated. Ditto for any tempo and dynamic markings. Some pianists charge extra for this service; some will charge according to their regular hourly rate. Remember that once the music is done properly, it is yours for-ever; so if the cost factor is amortized over the time you spend using the music, you'll find that it costs very little to have it prepared correctly.

Because of time restrictions at many auditions, you may be asked to sing only sixteen bars of a song. Plan for this by picking the sixteen bars of your favorite audition song that make a complete statement lyrically and musically. If the top notes of your range are strong, you may want to select the part of the piece that contains the highest notes. Rehearse the sixteen-bar section complete with a *short* introduction and an ending as if it were an entire song. And mark the music so it is clear where the starting place and finish are for the abbreviated version.

Ask your coach to show you what has been done to the music so that you can coherently explain it to others. When I work with singers, I tell them specifically what to say regarding all of the above points, then we rehearse them. And don't accept a line from your accompanist like, "Don't worry, I'll always play for you." One day he won't be available and you'll be stuck. There's no reason in the world you shouldn't know everything about your music.

Your coach should allow you to make a cassette tape of the accompaniments to your songs so that you can practice on your own. Don't ever work with someone who refuses to do this. You must practice your songs often, especially during long periods between auditions. If you have songs on tape, you can always keep your material freshly prepared and keep yourself in shape to sing without spending extra money for coaching every time there's an audition. And even if money isn't the problem, auditions often crop up at the last minute and you might not be able to coordinate schedules with your coach or with your accompanist.

Make sure you run through your song at least once, preferably several times, on the day of the audition. To make myself clearer, let me stress that at no time should your actual audition be the first time you sing on that particular day. Recently, I auditioned four women for the leading role in a musical concert. One woman showed up declaring that she hadn't warmed up that day and that she would sound better if she had. Well, how could the composer and I know how much better she would have sounded? We had no frame of reference for the quality of her voice. She did not get the role. Would she have gotten it if she had warmed up? Who knows. But she definitely would have been judged according to her performance-level qualifications.

If you happen to be doing a bit of traveling for the express purpose of auditioning (such as flying from one coast to another), please make sure that built into your travel schedule is adequate time for music rehearsal, whether with a vocal coach or with a tape. Most often, the airfare and accommodations will be at your own expense. I strongly urge you never to undertake the financial inconvenience of a long-distance audition (or any audition for that matter) if you cannot prepare properly, and a coast-to-coast journey is no excuse for showing up without either music or vocal warm-up. Just your mere physical presence is not enough to ensure your getting hired. If you can't audition at your very best, don't schedule an appointment!

PREPARATION—PART III: PERFORMING

WHEN TO BRING YOUR OWN PIANIST

Because of monetary considerations the answer to this one depends to a great extent on how much the job means to you. Now I know that most people who try out for a job hope to get it as a result of the audition. So if this book is all about minimizing the risks and maximizing your effectiveness, my advice would be that if you are auditioning for a featured role as opposed to a chorus job in a Broadway show or with a national touring company you should *always* bring your own pianist and find some way of working it out financially.

But I have to clarify that last statement a bit. The pianist you bring must be one with whom you have worked and who knows your material. I have seen more than one person come in to an audition with a pianist in tow and declare, "I just found out about this and only had enough time to call the pianist to get here in time. We haven't worked through the songs yet." As far as I am concerned, that is a waste of money. The hired pianist winds up playing the music while seeing it for the first time, and usually ends up transposing at sight, the same as the staff pianist would. So there is no advantage for the performer.

Yes, I too have heard of auditions where the staff pianist was not up to snuff and word—and panic—spread among the hopefuls. This is the only case in which there is the slightest excuse for the situation in the previous paragraph; and this does not occur often. Most of the audition pianists, especially in New York, are skilled, talented, patient people who truly want you to look good.

I am aware that most people simply can't afford to spend the money to bring their own pianist every time they audition; which makes it inexcusable not to have one's music in perfect condition so that it can be played easily by anyone at any time. But if you are auditioning with difficult or special material that has many changes of rhythm and tempo that demand perfect synchronization between the music and the voice, you must not expect any pianist, no matter how facile he is, to be able to give you the support that someone who knows the piece and has rehearsed it with you can.

I once played piano for the auditions of an Off-Broadway musical and in walked a woman none of us in the room knew, but whom we were all looking forward to seeing. This was a woman whose work was known to us and who stood a better-than-average chance of getting the part she was up for based on her proven talent.

She brought in a song that she had sung in a flop musical on Broadway some years before. The song was unknown to me. The music was in manuscript, in smeared pencil, with no lyrics anywhere on the pages. A few tempo indications were barely decipherable, and there were several sets of chords above each measure—a sign that she had performed this piece in several different keys.

But she had no idea which key was the most current, or even which key she wished to sing it in that day. She was used to having her own pianist, who knew all her music, come with her to auditions; so she wasn't able to communicate anything to me before having to sing. "Just follow me," she said impatiently. I did—and badly. I couldn't read the music, and because there were no lyrics, I couldn't be sure we were ever in the same place at the same time. It was truly my most frustrating experience ever at the piano.

She compounded the felony by being exceedingly rude to me in front of the director and choreographer, degrading me and my abilities because I was unable to play her music properly. Needless to say, she brought nothing else with her to sing—"My pianist has all my music"—and the outcome was also unsurprising: she not only didn't get the part; her behavior negated any chance of a callback.

But what should she have done under those circumstances?

She actually had several choices—all better than the one she picked. She could have tried to postpone or change her audition to a time when her own pianist would have been available. Or she could have found someone else with whom she could have worked beforehand to play for her. Or she could have found something simpler to sing. She also could have phoned me to suggest working with her the night before—she could have gotten my number from her agent or from the casting director of the show. She is a talented lady and has worked, to great acclaim, since that unfortunate afternoon; so she must've gotten it all together at some point afterwards.

SINGING THE RIGHT KIND OF SONG

If you've done your homework, as I outlined earlier, you now have a potent—and full—song portfolio. How do you know which songs to sing for which audition?

It is extremely important that you know what kind of show you are auditioning for. Is it contemporary? Rock? Traditional? Old-fashioned? Country-Western? A revival? Each would have very different types of music and therefore different requirements for singers. If your agent is the one who is arranging for the audition, your agent should be the one who informs you of anything special the production team might be asking for. If you get to the audition and find out that you have not been properly prepared, it is your responsibility to raise hell with whomever set up your appointment. You have the right to be adequately briefed. If it is indeed your agent who is at fault, don't let it happen more than once; change your agent as soon as possible.

Under ideal conditions, pick a song that is in the same period and style as the show. Don't make yourself crazy trying to match the score exactly. All I want to bring to your attention is that if you are auditioning for a traditional Broadway musical, it won't do you much good to sing a song written by the Rolling Stones. Or if you are auditioning for a Country-Western show, it is inappropriate to sing a Victor Herbert aria.

If your song portfolio consists of a number of different songs from several styles and periods, you won't ever be in the uncomfortable position of having to learn a new song overnight because you have just gotten an audition for which you don't have anything suitable.

Jerry Herman cautions: "Don't learn a new song for each audition. The best auditions I have listened to are by people who have been doing the same material for years and years. There's nothing that can replace the comfort of a song that you have been singing and feel secure with. So many people who came to the *La Cage aux Folles* auditions prepared something French or something they thought had a French sound, not realizing that we just wanted to hear their voices. Don't underestimate the imaginations of the people who are sitting out there in the dark. They really only need to hear what sounds best on you."

Lyricist Sheldon Harnick (*Fiorello!, She Loves Me, Fiddler on the Roof*) remembers an audition for one of his shows at which the stage manager came out and announced the next performer, someone with an African name. Out walked a tall, majestic-looking young black man carrying a Conga drum. He was wearing what appeared to be colorful African ceremonial robes, which made him look like a tribal chief. He strode to center stage, put the drum in front of him, and struck it several times with the palm of his hand. Mr. Harnick and his cohorts were primed for some wild, stirring, primitive chant. Instead, in a high nasal tenor, the actor launched into "On The Street Where You Live," a capella, except for an occasional blow to the drum. The effect was so ludicrously incongruous that those watching the audition could only laugh—it was impossible for them to evaluate the performer's talent. P.S. The man wasn't trying to be funny!

AT THE AUDITION:
DO'S AND DON'T'S—HINTS AND SECRETS

A lovely and talented singer-actress I have worked with confided to me she conquered her panic over auditioning by thinking of each audition as a performance. She said that if she adds up all the auditions she does in a year, it amounts to quite a lot of performing time. So in a way, she has psyched herself to the point where she actually looks forward to auditioning.

Did you ever hear the famous Noel Coward story? It seems there was a woman who showed up at the casting call for every show Mr. Coward did—musicals, straight plays, and revues. She always appeared well dressed, but her singing left lots to be desired. After many years, Mr. Coward, in deference to her tenacity rather than her talent, stepped up to the edge of the stage and said, "I'm very happy to tell you that at last we have a part for you." "Oh, no, Mr. Coward," she said, "I don't take parts. I just audition." And she grandly swept out.

No matter how prepared you are physically or emotionally, auditioning is a nervewracking business for most people. And nerves have to be the cause of some of the awkward actions actors engage in. Hence, another list of do's and don't's, with accompanying explanations:

1. Take the same advice your mother gave you before a long car trip: Use the rest room before you are called in to perform.

2. No matter how unimportant the job may seem at the time, *always* take auditions seriously. Always do your best. You never know what's going to happen in the future. Some people have long memories, and some have short. Assume that the people you audition for fall into the former category.

3. No matter what else you've had to do before the audition, pull yourself together somewhere outside of the place where the auditions are being held. Always remember that you are in a spotlight from the moment you are seen by any member of the production team of the show. If you walk into the room, or even the audition area, dishevelled and "spacey," it will be difficult later on to erase that first impression.

4. Auditions are notoriously off-schedule. You will most likely have to wait for some period of time before you are called. Instead of sitting there worrying, there are several things you can do to pass the time: Go over the songs you plan to sing, read a book, do a crossword puzzle—anything to help relieve the anxiety. Often you will know some of the others whose scheduled audition times are just before or just after yours, so you can spend a pleasant few minutes chatting with old friends or making new ones.

5. There's an important question you should ask the person who checks you in and that is, "For whom will I be auditioning?" By asking this, you will know how many people you will be facing—the number can vary from one person to as many as a dozen or so—and which members of the pro-

duction team will be present. You are well within your rights to know this information. The roster of people will change with every audition. For musicals, there will most often be a director, a choreographer, a musical director—who either will conduct the orchestra or play the piano during performances—and a producer, more than likely, several. When you audition for a new show in New York, you can expect the writers to be present. In some cases there will be assistants, friends, wives, husbands, and even lovers of the various aforementioned participants.

6. If you arrive later than your appointed time, it is usually unnecessary to offer any kind of excuse for your lateness. Everyone is aware of the unpredictability of public transportation and the unreliability of taxicabs in city traffic. It's not uncommon for actors to be seen in an order different from the planned schedule. If many people are auditioned in a day, the director and his cohorts are usually not aware that you *are* late until you tell them. I don't mean to condone lateness, but if you find yourself unavoidably late, just be composed when you enter the room and say nothing. If you are asked, take the advice Michael Shurtleff gives in his book *Audition,* which is to lie, saying, "I was detained at another audition" rather than offering such excuses as, "I had to take my ferret to the vet this morning and it threw me off schedule all day." (See Appendix B for more advice regarding excuses.)

7. Leave your disappointments and anxieties outside the audition area. At the chorus auditions for the original production of *The Music Man,* one fellow came in and sang his sixteen bars. As with everybody else, the director, Morton DaCosta, didn't have time to say anything but "Thank you very much." The actor walked down to the footlights and

said, "That's easy for *you* to say, you son-of-a-bitch!" and harangued Mr. DaCosta for several minutes until he was dragged off the stage. Obviously the actor was frustrated by several failed auditions. You must, to the best of your ability, leave all of that behind and forget the ogres who are out front. Your attitude must "read" success, not failure.

8. Do figure out what you are going to sing *before* you enter the audition room. You'll be a lot calmer if you have that planned ahead of time. It happens fairly frequently that the director asks what you brought, and after you rattle off the list, he may ask you to sing something other than what would have been your first choice. If the decision is yours, sing your most exciting song first; sing the song you would do if you were only going to sing one number. In addition, have your music—and your picture and resume—ready in your hands before entering the room; don't search through your bags while everyone waits.

Make sure that you are familiar and comfortable with whatever music you bring with you to the audition. If you don't have with you the music for a song you performed only once ten years ago, and whose words you don't really remember all that well, you won't be tempted to use it if you're asked to sing an extra song.

9. When you enter the audition room, try not to come in with all your personal belongings—if you have a coat, a dance bag, a purse, or a spare pair of shoes, you immediately convey a bag-lady image. It is usually possible to leave your things in the waiting area and ask one of the other people auditioning to keep an eye on them while you are inside. If you must bring your bags and coat in with you, place them right beside the door so they can be grabbed

quickly on your way out—it makes for the swiftest and most graceful exit. Do not under any circumstances place your things on the same table the director uses. Don't laugh, people have done that! If the audition is on a stage, leave your things at the edge of the proscenium arch, and, if possible, out of sight of the audience.

10. When you are ushered into your performing area, your name will be announced and, if you have not brought your own pianist, you should proceed directly to the piano. If you *have* brought your own accompanist, he should go to the piano and you should go to your performance space. Sometimes you will be introduced to the people observing the audition, sometimes not. If you are not personally introduced, don't ask "Who are you?" of anyone. If you didn't ask outside, you can question the staff pianist about who is who.

11. Don't try to engage the director or writers in "ice-breaker" conversation. Excessive chatting is almost always counter-productive. Although you're trying to be charming and friendly—and attempting to ease your own nerves before you sing—it rarely comes off quite that smoothly. It can seem intrusive and, in truth, just slows things down. I know it sounds harsh, but the rule "Don't speak unless you're spoken to" seems to be a good one to follow.

And for heaven's sake, don't offer any sob stories to the production staff. One woman *always* comes in with a story on the order of "I really have to do this show because my son is going to college in the fall and I need the tuition." I'm sure her reasons are true. But nobody will hire her out of sympathy. Her remarks have always provoked the opposite reaction—I heard the comments made after she left the room. They were not full of warmth and compassion. It's much better to let your talent do the talking.

12. If the audition is in a room, rather than a theatre, pick a spot to sing from that is near—but not right next to—the piano and that is also a comfortable distance away from the people watching. That distance is important and allows those observing to approximate the way you would look onstage. Since you will want to move a bit while you sing, as opposed to standing like a statue, do so laterally—sideways. Do not creep forward toward the casting team. Moving toward those auditioning you can intimidate and make them uncomfortable.

13. If you are in a theatre, this next point is not a concern, but in a studio you have to be aware of where you look while you sing. Most people advise you not to look directly at the people auditioning you so as not to challenge them with the lyrics to the song. You should focus on a spot just over their heads. But pick at least one short phrase that can be sung right to one of the members of the casting team. The phrase should be informational in content—not something that either threatens or requires an answer from the listener.

14. Don't use props while you audition. Even depending on a chair to be present can cause problems in some audition rooms, and also takes time to set up. It is very important for the director to see how you use your body when you sing, so sitting in a chair somewhat defeats the purpose. Don't depend on the piano to lean on or refer to. What if your audition is on a stage and the piano is in the pit? It's better to stay as self-contained as possible. And as flexible as possible.

Speaking of props, there was a young man who came to auditions carrying his rather large teddy bear. He never let go of the bear and even held it close to him when he sang. He probably carried it for the same reason children hold security blankets. But the bear was never referred to in the guy's song. Once, the director was grouping people by type and this young man was one of ten lined up—only to the director's surprise there were eleven faces in the row.

15. If the director suddenly asks you to perform your song in a manner different from the way you are used to, don't fight him or resist. Make an honest attempt to follow the instructions, even if you think you look or sound foolish. The director is obviously trying to see how adaptable you are and how speedily you can absorb new ideas. You will get extra brownie points if you show you are willing to go out on a limb.

16. Don't ask the question "Do you want me to sing two songs?" either before or after you do your first one. Everyone in the room assumes you have brought more than one, so the best procedure is to pause after your first song and wait for some response. Either you will be asked to sing something else or you will be told something like "Thank you, that song showed us everything we needed to hear," in which case you should politely make preparations to leave the room. Don't put them on the spot. The remark that sounds like a brush-off may not be. Most trained listeners can tell after the first sixteen bars how well you sing, and one song may indeed be sufficient for them to determine whether or not you fit in with the specific needs of the show.

HOW TO TALK TO THE PIANIST
AND WHAT TO SAY

If you are not bringing your own accompanist, the staff pianist provided by the production is—usually—your only friend in the audition room. Since, as I said earlier, he is there to serve you, there are things you must do to give him the greatest possible chance to play your music with as much assurance as your own pianist would. But remember, no pianist can be expected to be a mind reader and correctly guess at your interpretation.

Thus, the first rule: Take your time at the piano. Even if the audition is running behind, you will be allowed a few moments to explain the routine, tempo, and feeling of your song to the pianist.

I am assuming at this point that your music is legible and transposed, and that the introduction and the ending, as well as any tempo and dynamic markings, are clearly indicated. If this is the case, you will not need more than about twenty seconds to point out some of the tricky spots.

It is imperative that you give the pianist a clear idea of the tempo. Do this by softly singing a few measures of the song to him at the speed you wish to perform it.

In brief, here are the four things to tell a pianist:

1. The key

2. Where to start

3. Where to stop

4. How fast to play

Also, don't treat the pianist like a human extension of the piano. Remember the old barroom sign, "Please don't shoot the piano player—he's doing the best he can"? The audition pianists really do try to support you properly. Considering the horrendous state of most of the music they must play from, they do a yeoman's work in accompanying sometimes up to a hundred people a day. After you are done, it is courteous to say, "Thank you." Take it from me, it is noticed by everyone in the room.

WHAT TO DO IF YOU FORGET THE LYRICS

In two words: Keep calm. It happens more often than anyone realizes. Maybe in one out of every ten auditions. It is not the end of the world. Naturally no one would ever wish for it to happen, but if it does, your aplomb in dealing with it can turn what seems like a disaster into quite a victory for you.

Once again, don't try to make excuses. They are not necessary and almost always make you look bad.

People most often forget lyrics when they aren't fully concentrating on what they are doing. Don't let your mind wander, no matter how many times you have performed that particular song. Keep it fresh.

But if you should suddenly go blank and can't remember what word comes next, you can simply turn to the pianist, who will throw you the lyric so you can continue. If the lyrics are not on the music, that truly *is* a disaster, and you should immediately go back to the section entitled "How to Prepare Your Music" and memorize it.

Even singing la-la-la is all right until you remember the words—if it is a short lapse. Listen to Judy Garland singing "You Go To My Head" on her live "Judy at Carnegie Hall" album. Yes,

Judy Garland forgot the lyrics. A big star. At Carnegie Hall, yet. And preserved forever on a best-selling phonograph record. But she handled it with her marvelous sense of humor. Brilliantly.

You can, as Judy did, sing *anything* over the notes. If you think quickly on your feet and are entertaining enough, you'll get away with it.

THE OPEN CALL

The first professional audition most people encounter will probably be an "open call"—commonly referred to as a "cattle call." At this time you will be one of hundreds competing for just a mere handful of whatever chorus positions are available.

Open call means just that—it is open to anyone who wishes to be seen and considered. You probably will have to stand on a long line in order to put your name at the end of a lengthy list of contenders. Sometimes, before even getting a chance to sing, people are "typed out"—that is, only those who have the right look for the show are asked to stay. A frustrating situation, but don't let it discourage you. Keep going to these kinds of auditions. Eventually you will be allowed to show your stuff.

Because of the sheer numbers of people who show up to be auditioned at an open call, you will rarely be permitted to sing an entire song. Instead, you will usually be asked to sing sixteen bars of any song with which you are familiar and comfortable. An accompanist is almost always provided.

Follow the instructions precisely! Don't ask the accompanist to do more than sixteen bars, even if the song is very fast or very short. He is bound by the same time constraints you are, and must carry out the wishes of the production staff. If you are requested to sing a ballad, don't do an up-tune, and vice versa. Of course, you should be able to perform the whole song all the way through if you are asked—but *only* if you are asked!

Don't be put off if you have to sing in front of the others auditioning. Because of time considerations, it is sometimes more expedient to keep everyone in the audition room while one by one you are called upon to perform. This often happens in professional dance calls. It is an uncomfortable situation, but remember that everyone feels the same way and the production staff is aware of it. But the performers who appear the most fearless and who do the best under the peer pressure will have an edge over the competition.

Although—as you know by now only too well—I have gone through great pains to convince you to perform little-known material, in the open-call situation it is not vitally important to knock yourself out finding an obscure song. You may sing something well-known. What matters here is to make the best impression as quickly as possible. Sing something that shows off your vocal prowess. If you look right and sound right, you will stand out.

SUMMER STOCK

If you are auditioning for a part in a summer stock production, it is essential that you familiarize yourself with the show—or shows, if you are auditioning for the whole season of productions the theatre is doing. You should find out what the roles in the shows require in terms of age, look, and type, as well as what songs those characters sing.

Along with your standard audition material, you should prepare the songs sung by the characters for which you may be considered. In the current economic situation, most summer stock theatres or dinner theatres are struggling financially; so it is folly on your part to audition for the role of, say, Lois Lane in *Kiss Me, Kate* if you are a soprano. The theatres simply do not have the money to transpose the standard orchestrations, let alone have the songs rescored, no matter how much they want you in their production.

You should have prepared not only the actual show songs, but also at least one song that is *similar* to the real songs. When you get to the audition, ask the person who checks off your name when you arrive if those hearing the auditions are asking for songs from the show or if they are asking for other material. This way you can be mentally prepared and you won't have to ask once you are in the room. If the person outside doesn't know, ask the pianist what others have been doing. If you've taken my advice, you'll be ready either way—and in an especially good position if you sing a song of your choosing, which interests the production team, and then are asked to sing from the show. If you have readied the song beforehand, you could secure yourself the part in those few minutes. If you fumble, the last impression you leave will not be the best.

Most summer stock theatres and dinner theatres do fairly standard-fare presentations, so the libretti and scores—as well as recordings—are widely available in libraries and theatre book stores.

Once again, there's no substitute for preparation. You'll have an edge over those unprepared.

AT THE CALLBACK

Final casting decisions are never made in the first round of auditions. During that time, the people doing the casting are making special note of anyone who could possibly fill the roles in the show. These actors are given a callback—which is just another chance to audition on a different day. Most often the callback is scheduled within a week of the first audition. However, there have been cases of callbacks being scheduled months later. If you have been selected for a return visit, it means that you are under serious consideration.

There are certain accepted practices for callbacks:

1. Wear the same clothes you wore to the first audition. You were called back because your talent and your appearance were liked sufficiently to warrant a second look. If you dress or fashion your hair differently you may look entirely wrong to the production team and thus do yourself a disservice.

2. The same goes for songs. Bring the same two songs you sang the first time. But it is imperative that you bring additional material. Once again, your song portfolio can come in handy at the callback—the director may want to see you display colors other than the ones you showed previously.

It is permissible at this juncture to ask if you should sing a different song or do the one you sang the last time. Since, as I mentioned earlier, the casting people wrote down what you did at the first audition, they will welcome being given the option.

If it is *your* choice, my previous advice holds: Sing the flashiest, most exciting song in your repertoire. Since you don't know if they will want a second number—*and don't ask!*—do as your first number the one you would pick if you were told you would only sing one song.

Once again, if, when you are in the room, you are suddenly asked to do a certain type of song you have not prepared, for heaven's sake don't attempt to fumble through something you may only half-know. Don't ever try to perform when you are not ready. If you do, the last impression you leave with the production team will be one of sloppiness. If you have a parcel of songs to choose from and are still asked to do something else, it is not bad form to say, "I'm sorry, I don't have anything like that under my belt. If you'd like, I could work up that kind of song and come in again." Most often, you will not have to learn anything new, although you may be asked to return for a second callback. If you do get a special request, try to get from the director—or whoever is doing the asking—as specific an assignment as possible, so that when you return, you will be doing precisely what they thought they wanted.

A TOUCH OF THE OUTRAGEOUS

I tremble a bit to include this topic for fear of its consequences. Throwing caution to the winds, I dutifully mention that some performers have gotten some mileage out of their auditions by being slightly outrageous.

On a recent *Tonight Show* on television, director-choreographer Tommy Tune (*Nine, My One and Only*) described to guest-hostess Joan Rivers how he auditioned in his performing days: While he sang the song "M-O-T-H-E-R"—"M is for the million things she gave me . . ."—he twisted his tall, lanky body to form the letters M,O,T,H,E,R. Ms. Rivers asked Mr. Tune if he would hire a person who came in to audition and did that same routine. Mr. Tune said yes, because it would show him that the actor had some imagination and a sense of humor.

Two of the most quoted stories in recent memory involve Mary Jo Catlett. Now well-known for her appearances on Raid commercials and for her role as Pearl on television's *Diff'rent Strokes,* Ms. Catlett had, by the time the first incident described below took place, already been on Broadway in *Hello, Dolly!* among other shows.

She, like many other performers, had a fear of auditioning—translation: fear of rejection—and it took her some time to conquer it. When she did, she too treated the audition as if she were performing a part in a play. Then it became great fun for her, and she went to just about any lengths to get a part—especially if she knew in advance something about the show.

In 1971, at the time her appointment was scheduled by the casting director for the Broadway musical *Different Strokes*—no relation to the similarly named television show—Ms. Catlett was asked to prepare a song and sing it as if hung over. After due consideration, she picked a song that would suggest the opposite of how one would feel in that condition: "I Feel Pretty" from *West Side Story*. In the audition room she put three chairs together, laid down on them on her back, and sang. After the first quatrain, she rolled over and fell flat on the floor and continued singing, face down. She got the part.

Another story involving Ms. Catlett falls into the Chutzpah Department. For the Broadway revival of *The Pajama Game,* which was to be directed by the show's original director, George Abbott, she auditioned for the part of the executive secretary, Mabel, and didn't hear anything after her audition. Through the grapevine she found out that the producers were on the brink of hiring someone else but weren't enthusiastic about their choice. She got a call to go back and audition again as if she had never been there before. It was suggested that she wear a blonde wig—she is a brunette—and sing a different song; because if she did, in theory, Mr. Abbott would never know she was the same woman he wasn't interested in earlier. She took the suggestion and got the job, although she's convinced she didn't fool the ever-wise Mr. Abbott. P.S. She didn't have to wear the wig in the show.

The funniest audition I ever witnessed was for *Trixie True, Teen Detective*. The director asked everyone to bring a comedy number. Almost half of the men brought the song "Floozies" from *The Grass Harp*—an amusing song, but not really comic.

One man, tall, rugged, and very masculine in a natural, self-assured way, had us all in stitches when he sang "I Enjoy Being a Girl" from *Flower Drum Song* in his rich baritone without any camping whatsoever.

It's a fine line, but if you can find a way to make yourself stand out by doing something extraordinarily different, try it. A word of caution: First try it out on several of your more staid friends before you gamble at an audition. If you're at all in doubt as to the true humor of your plan, stick to something safe.

AFTER THE AUDITION

So now you've been conscientious, done all the preparation, and worked your tail off. You've also just done an audition and you feel, well, strange. Perhaps a little let down. It's natural. Perhaps your thoughts fall into one of the following categories:

1. I have no idea how it went.

2. I was terrible—they're never going to hire me.

3. I was terrific—but they didn't seem the least bit interested.

4. I was terrific—I'm sure I'm going to get cast.

Within reason, you should be able to tell how well you sang and/or danced, and how comfortable you felt as a performer, but that's about all. You cannot accurately measure the reactions of the production team. Even if they talked and ate sandwiches during your audition—which is rude on their part, but it's done—you shouldn't take that as a certain sign of a negative attitude towards you.

The only thing you should think after an audition is:

5. I gave a great audition. Even if I don't get cast I know they saw me at my best.

So if you think your audition left room for improvement, try to figure out why so that you can correct the problems next time.

Most importantly, if you think you did well but still didn't get cast, don't start to think you are terrible or untalented. There are too many variables out of your control in an audition situation which include the specific requirements of the show and the particular preferences of the creative team. You can't—and therefore shouldn't try to—second-guess what is on their minds as they listen to you. And if you have heard any "inside" information from other actors, you should only listen with one ear: your actor colleagues constantly exchange misinformation and are not , necessarily reliable sources.

Another factor most people are unaware of is that when shows currently running are looking for replacements, actors who fit the costumes and don't require transpositions can save a lot of money for the company. If you're the wrong size or vocal range, you're probably out of luck regardless of your talent and preparation.

Unfortunately, it is simply not possible for you to get feedback on how your audition went. If you thought you did everything right and got cut early, or didn't get at least a callback, you probably will never know why. The only thing you should ever be concerned with is taking charge of your own presentation and demonstrating your talent in the most satisfactory way possible. Don't blame the world for not recognizing your true genius; the place to look is within yourself. Whatever you may be doing wrong *can* be corrected.

But once in a great while, one of the members of the production team may just have it in for you, and your audition, no matter how good, may be doomed before you start, as happened at the following audition:

Several years ago in New York City, all the people awaiting their turn to sing—about twenty—were invited to sit on little chairs on the stage to watch the other auditions. In the group was the girl friend of one of the producers. She had been flown in from Los Angeles by her producer-friend to try out, and was tastefully and becomingly attired in a black sheath with a strand of pearls around her neck. When her name was announced, she gave her music to the staff pianist and in a soprano voice sang "And This Is My Beloved." Beautifully. A nasty little voice from out front said, "Miss, you know that's not the right kind of song for our show. Do you have anything to *belt?*" Composed, she turned to the pianist and said, "I'll do 'Johnny One-Note'—start in D then move up to E-flat." And she told him at which point to modulate. She blew the roof off the theatre. She was so terrific, in fact, that afterwards, everyone on stage spontaneously applauded her. Up from the audience came the man who had spoken earlier—the director. On the stage, in front of everyone, he said, "Miss, I know you're from the Coast, but first of all, your choice of material is terrible. You must never wear a black velvet sheath, and pearls are outclassed. Now tell me, *what have you done before?*" Summoning up all the dignity she could muster after that gratuitous humiliation, she said, "Well, in the beginning, I created heaven and earth."

Whatever your particular experience may be, always remember the words of the late Lehman Engel: "Rejection at an audition is not the conclusion of anything, only the end of a single exploration."

Keep plugging.

Try new things.

Keep auditioning.

You'll get there. Talent will out.

APPENDICES

APPENDIX A

A PARTIAL LIST OF THE MOST OVERDONE AUDITION SONGS

If you are using any song on this list, please immediately find a substitute. If you are saying now, "But I use that song and I always get jobs with it," I'm truly happy to be proved wrong in your case—but you are an anomaly.

Songs also appear on this list for more than just the reason that they are overdone. Songs such as the brilliant tour de force "Crossword Puzzle" are way too long to use as audition pieces. And songs such as "All That Jazz" don't reveal enough about the performer, no matter how brilliantly they are done. Both types of songs should, as detailed in the main body of text in this book, not be considered ideal audition material.

Anyway, this list is current as of this writing. Songs seem to go in and out of vogue, and one month everyone will be doing the same song and, just as suddenly, the next month no one will bring it in. Use this list as a general guide to songs that have been used the most in the last few years.

Any song from *Jacques Brel*
All I Need Is The Girl (*Gypsy*)
All That Jazz (*Chicago*)
All The Things You Are (*Very Warm For May*)
Almost Like Being In Love (*Brigadoon*)
And This Is My Beloved (*Kismet*)
Anyone Can Whistle (*Anyone Can Whistle*)
Art Is Calling Me (*The Enchantress*)
A Wonderful Guy (*South Pacific*)
Be A Lion (*The Wiz*)
Being Alive (*Company*)
Cabaret (*Cabaret*)
Can't Help Lovin' Dat Man (*Show Boat*)
Corner Of The Sky (*Pippin*)
Crossword Puzzle (*Starting Here, Starting Now*)
Don't Tell Mama (*Cabaret*)
Everybody Says Don't (*Anyone Can Whistle*)
Everything's Coming Up Roses (*Gypsy*)
Extraordinary (*Pippin*)
Feelin' Good (*The Roar of the Greasepaint . . .*)
Glitter And Be Gay (*Candide*)
God Bless The Child
Gorgeous (*The Apple Tree*)
Her Face (*Carnival*)
Hit Me With A Hot Note (*Sophisticated Ladies*)
I Can Cook Too (*On The Town*)
Ice Cream (*She Loves Me*)
I Don't Remember Christmas (*Starting Here, Starting Now*)
If I Loved You (*Carousel*)
I Got Rhythm (*Girl Crazy*)
I'll Build A Stairway To Paradise (*George White's Scandals*)
I'll Never Fall In Love Again (*Promises, Promises*)
I Love A Piano (*Stop! Look! Listen!*)
I Met A Girl (*Bells Are Ringing*)

It Never Entered My Mind (*Higher and Higher*)

I Wish I Were In Love Again (*Babes In Arms*)

Joey, Joey, Joey (*The Most Happy Fella*)

Johnny One-Note (*Babes In Arms*)

Losing My Mind (*Follies*)

Love, I Hear (*A Funny Thing Happened On The Way To The Forum*)

Luck Be A Lady (*Guys and Dolls*)

Mama, A Rainbow (*Minnie's Boys*)

Maria (*West Side Story*)

Maybe (*Annie*)

Maybe This Time (*Cabaret*—movie)

Metaphor (*The Fantasticks*)

Moonfall (*The Mystery of Edwin Drood*)

Much More (*The Fantasticks*)

Nobody Does It Like Me (*Seesaw*)

Nothing (*A Chorus Line*)

Once Upon A Time (*All American*)

On My Own (*Fame*—movie)

On The Other Side Of The Tracks (*Little Me*)

On The Street Where You Live (*My Fair Lady*)

People (*Funny Girl*)

Promises, Promises (*Promises, Promises*)

Real Live Girl (*Little Me*)

She Loves Me (*She Loves Me*)

Soliloquy (*Carousel*)

Something's Coming (*West Side Story*)

Stranger In Paradise (*Kismet*)

Strong Woman Number (*I'm Getting My Act Together . . .*)

The Greatest Love Of All (*The Greatest*—movie)

The Impossible Dream (*Man of La Mancha*)

The Joker (*The Roar of the Greasepaint . . .*)

They Call The Wind Maria (*Paint Your Wagon*)

They Were You (*The Fantasticks*)

Tomorrow (*Annie*)
Tonight At Eight (*She Loves Me*)
Try Me (*She Loves Me*)
Wait Till You See Her (*By Jupiter*)
What I Did For Love (*A Chorus Line*)
Where Am I Going? (*Sweet Charity*)
Why Can't I Walk Away? (*Maggie Flynn*)
Younger Than Springtime (*South Pacific*)
Your Feet's Too Big (*Ain't Misbehavin'*)

It's also a good idea to avoid brand new hit songs. Even before *Cats* opened on Broadway too many singers performed "Memory" at auditions, each one thinking that they would be the only one to be doing it at that point in time. Play it safer with little-known older material. There's tons of it to choose from!

APPENDIX B

EXCUSES, EXCUSES

All of you who think you are being original when you offer an explanation as to why you are not at your best at an audition, please think again. Every possible excuse has been offered too many times. And they are all incredibly self-defeating. I'd be filthy rich if I had a dollar for every time the following had been said:

I have a cold.

I have just recovered from a cold.

I feel a cold coming on.

I didn't have any music to sing so I just stopped at the music store and bought this song. How does it go?

I just found out about the audition this morning, so I couldn't prepare adequately.

My pianist has my music.

I'm not warmed up.

I had a long night (rough night, heavy gig, hot date, etc.) last night.

I just got into town.

I'm in the process of moving—or, I have just moved—so my music isn't in good shape.

I just learned this song yesterday.

I learned this song from the record, but I never heard the accompaniment before.

It's too early to sing—my voice isn't warmed up.
(Said at every audition before noon.)

Please note that a once-popular excuse is not heard much anymore: "My dog chewed up my music." I don't know whether the disappearance of this excuse means that more actors have cats than have dogs, or that maybe there are just better-trained canines around.

APPENDIX C

TAPING YOUR MUSIC

Now I realize that it may sound incredibly picky, but there is a right way and a wrong way to tape music together. Since it is just as easy to tape it either way, please try the method I describe.

Let's assume you have a four-page song with music printed on only one side of each sheet. Take pages 1 and 2 and lay them flat on a table facing you, with page 2 to the right of page 1. The first trick here is to leave a small hairline space between the pages. This is to allow for the thickness of the tape when you fold the pages—the result is that the music folds flat and opens flat. Put tape down the front of the music only. Use three pieces of tape rather than one long one. This is done so that if one piece splits down the center, the other two are still there hanging in.

To attach page 3 requires a second trick. You put page 3 to the right of page 2, leaving the hairline space between the pages; but this time you attach the tape from the *back* side of the music only. This is so that when you fold the music, the sticky part of the tape is always on the *inside* of the fold.

Now as for page 4, place it to the right of page 3, leaving the space between the pages, and put the tape, once again, on the front.

You fold the music by leaving page 1 facing you on the front, with the other pages arranged accordian-style. Page 4 will face you on the back. Voila, you're done.

If the song has five pages, follow the instructions for page 3. If any of this sounds confusing, it'll all make lots of sense when you try your first one.

APPENDIX D

YOUR PHOTO AND RESUME

Until that pie-in-the-sky day arrives when you achieve stardom, you will need to have current pictures and up-to-date resumes ready to give to anyone who may cast you in anything. So, as promised earlier, here are a few observations on that ubiquitous duo.

Note to newcomers: The trade papers are full of ads for photographers and for resume-typing services. If you don't have one that is personally recommended, shop around, compare prices and the quality of the work. Then, if you have to, draw straws and pick one.

First and foremost, your picture and resume should be attached. There's nothing that looks more unprofessional than carrying them around unattached. Spend a few minutes at home pasting the resumes to the backs of the photographs, using rubber cement.

Don't present a packet of reviews and clippings at an audition. The people evaluating the auditions don't have time to read them—neither when you are in the room nor later on. Nor are they the least bit interested in doing so. All the great things that have been said about you in print will do no earthly good if you make a poor showing in person.

Keep your resume to one page. If you have so many credits that it takes more than one page to list them all, just put the more important ones down. Or make up two separate resumes, each geared to different types of work, i.e., one that lists all your theatrical credits, and another that lists all your commercials and your industrial shows.

Don't make the resume too cluttered. You want your experience to be immediately comprehensible. In this regard, always list your more important credits first. Use this order as a guideline for your musical resume:

1. Broadway productions

2. National tours

3. Stock, regional, and dinner theatre productions

4. College productions

5. Film and television shows

Be factual. I remember one particular actor who listed he had worked for a particular director. Unfortunately, he was auditioning that day for the director named—and the director was certain he had never worked with that actor. My point is: *Don't fabricate credits.* If you're worried that your resume looks unimpressive, don't worry. If you're talented, your credits will grow quickly enough.

Never put any unnecessary information on the resume. At an audition I played at some years ago an actress presented her resume, and after her less-than-impressive audition it was immediately consigned to the trash basket. I retrieved it, kept it, and still have it in my files because it was so bizarre. On it was written: "My most exciting experience was natural childbirth. However, it's hardly marketable."

As for your photo, make sure it is recent and that it looks like you. You always want a flattering photograph, but it is important that your picture resemble the person standing in front of those casting the show. After you leave the room, your photo is all they have to remember you by. The picture *must* call to mind the actor the casting people just saw.

A surprising number of women have had composite photo resumes done containing pictures of themselves in the nude. This is certainly an attention-getting device and it does work. The resumes do stand out from the others and are often kept by the male members of the production team. They are also frequently tacked up on office walls. But the ladies are *never* seriously considered for roles. Unless, maybe, for *Oh, Calcutta!*

You should always carry a few photos and resumes around with you wherever you go. You may be asked for an extra at an audition or you may run into someone else there—another director, or perhaps a casting agent—who could have a use for one. It doesn't weigh that much to take a handful with you. And the one time you don't have an extra is the time you'll be asked for one.

APPENDIX E

TO AGENT OR NOT TO AGENT

And Other Questions Answered

As I mentioned earlier, it is difficult to secure an audition for a principal role in a Broadway show unless you are recommended by a reputable theatrical agent. So how do you go about getting an agent to represent you? I posed this and other questions to Jeffrey Dunn, a New York based casting director, when he was an agent in the Musical Theatre department of the Fifi Oscard agency. (What follows is an edited version of that interview.)

When Mr. Dunn and I spoke, Actors' Equity (the union to which all professional theatre performers must belong) rulings made it extraordinarily hard for non-Equity performers to be auditioned for any productions having a contract with that union. This encompasses all Broadway shows, off-Broadway shows, national touring companies, bus and truck tours, and most professional companies across the nation. After June 1, 1988 the ruling changed, and all performers who satisfy certain criteria, whether members of Equity or not, will be treated in the same manner with regard to the scheduling of auditions.*

QUESTION: But aren't your chances of getting cast better if you are a full-fledged member of Equity?

JEFFREY DUNN: If you've just arrived in town, I don't think the best idea is to get your Equity card immediately. Unless you're interested in being a chorus person for the rest of your life, you're better off getting roles under your belt in good non-Equity stock companies. If you're talented, it's quite possible you can get some really good parts that you wouldn't get in an Equity company for years. It's also a way to start making contacts and connections. Quite frequently the directors at those theatres do move into better things. The second-assistant stage manager of this year's dinner-theatre production could be directing a Broadway show in five years.

QUESTION: Where does someone find out about these theatres?

JD: There's a book published called the *Non-Equity Performer's SUMMER THEATRE GUIDE from an Actor's Viewpoint* by John Allen (see Appendix G for information on ordering). From interviews with people who have worked in them, the book discusses all the stock theatres: What the pay scale is like; what the living conditions are; whether people enjoy working there, etc. It's important to know this ahead of time, because when you're talking about non-Equity you're not covered by any rulings except public health, and that sometimes comes into play at some of these theatres.

---

* For the specific criteria and an application, write to Actors' Equity Association at their offices in New York, Chicago, or Los Angeles. Sending a stamped, self-addressed legal-size envelope along with your request will speed your reply.

Q: So for how long should a performer continue to do non-Equity work before he gets his Equity card?

JD: Remember that once you get your card, you can never act in a professional non-Equity production again without Equity's express permission. I know many young actors who, having finished a successful season of stock—doing nine musicals in nine weeks—think, "Now I'm ready! I want my Equity card!" They somehow get it within about a year and never get another Equity job again. Many promising careers grind to a halt as a result of getting the card. I see people all the time who come to me with resumes with one Equity credit and the rest is all nonunion, and not recent nonunion work at that, and I can't do a lot with them because they're competing with everybody who has ever been in a Broadway show or national tour. I think you should always be functioning on the level where you're competitive. Those who attend non-Equity open calls for Broadway shows and are not getting the jobs think, "All I need is to get my card and then I'll work." Do they really think that if they go to the same calls and compete with the Equity people they're going to get cast? That the letters A.E.A. next to their names will make them sound better? It won't. If you need an Equity card, you'll get it—and I've rarely seen somebody not get it when he was ready. But I've seen many people who got it when they weren't.

Q: When should performers get an agent?

JD: Again, when they're ready. An agent tends to work in the more important venues, the ones that are going to be income-producing or career-building. An agent is not going to be that interested in booking you for a summer in New Hampshire—making minimum doing interesting shows every week—or putting you in an Off-Off-Broadway musical, unless it seems to have the potential to move somewhere. There are many people who come to me who are very talented, but whom I don't think I can do a lot with yet because they are just so green. They don't have the experience. I'm reluctant to take on somebody that I can't get seen. Even with people who've been on Broadway—assuming that their agents have good reputations and good credibility—if casting directors don't know the actor's work it is sometimes difficult to get them seen for every project—or even for the ones they're right for. Be sure when you go after an agent that you have something to offer him other than just your talent. You have to have credentials that you were able to get on your own. Start looking as soon as you feel your talent is at a level where you can utilize an agent, but don't expect to be a signed client until agents are going to be able to keep you busy working. An agent is happiest when his clients are working.

It's never a bad thing at any point in your career to send a picture and resume to an agent with a note saying, "I'm not represented right now. Perhaps if you're interested, we can talk." Don't be crestfallen if they won't see you initially. And then if they'll meet with you but won't do anything for you, just keep in touch with them; let them know when you're doing things, and gradually, if they see that your career seems to be moving, they will jump on the bandwagon quickly. They'd be foolish not to. But when you first get to town, it's just important to work, because work begets work.

Q: Obviously, if an actor is working, he's also being seen and exposed to others in the business.

JD: Also, the people you meet and work with form a network where you exchange information. Although not always 100 percent reliable, it's a start in learning which director is good and which isn't; which agent is good, which isn't; whom you can trust, whom you can't; don't work at this theatre, and so on. From working, people know you. Even if they just see your name in a program, it's better than not. Your name should get to be familiar to people. But you shouldn't work in stuff that's not good. It's very possible to take mediocre material and make it wonderful, as many Tony Award winners who've been in mediocre musicals would bear out. But don't be involved in something that you would be embarrassed to invite people to. As important as it is to keep working, it's also important to keep an eye on the long term—that you're looking to build a career. Certainly, don't invite an agent to a show if you're the only good thing in it; don't make them spend an evening seeing a rotten show for your terrific five minutes. Better to drop them a note and say, "I'm doing this show and I think I'm very good in it, however, I don't think the rest of it is that good. If you're really interested in seeing me, come between 9:30 and 10:00, that's when I do my stuff." It's unlikely that the agent will come, but the fact that you had that much faith in your work and were considerate of the agent at the same time will not go unnoticed.

Q: Do agents scour the town going to showcases and the like looking for new talent?

JD: As with any group of people, you can't generalize. I do go out a lot to cover people for the areas I work in. However, one of the areas I work in is musicals. So I don't miss an important musical project anywhere.

Q: Do you approach people you like in shows to see if they're represented?

JD: Yes, definitely. If they say they're not represented, then I give them my card and tell them to call. And do you want to hear something amazing? Quite frequently they don't. Maybe they're afraid to call or they wonder if I really meant it. I don't give out my card if I don't want to hear from them, even at the risk of hurting somebody's feelings, which I hate to do, but I really won't lead people on. If you do good work and people see it, and they think that you have a big career, they're going to go up and talk to you afterwards. I think most agents would.

Q: Okay, you're an actor, and an agent has asked to see you. Should you sign with the agent?

JD: With some agents, the minute they meet you they want to sign you. You have to find the right agent. Signing with an agent is like a marriage. It's a relationship. You have to have good communication. I don't think that can happen in a fifteen-minute meeting; it can only happen in time. And it takes two for it to work well. For the agent, he needs to be sure that he can get you seen, that he can keep you busy. And you have to find out whether you're going to be submitted for things that you're right for and for the kinds of things you want to be doing. You can have a somewhat successful career without being signed with an agent. There are several people who have had Broadway careers but who, for one reason or another, are unsigned. Getting signed means finding an agent who knows what you do, likes what you do, and knows what to do with it. And that doesn't always happen. However, when you get to a certain point, you've got to have an agent or a manager, at least to do your contract negotiating.

Q: Any more general advice?

JD: You have to have the confidence in your own talent and your own ability—to know you're going to hit it, but to keep working on it and nurturing it like any growing thing. And the patience to put up with everything you have to put up with until that time comes without going crazy. You have to find things that you can do to keep yourself from getting nuts.

Q: Like what?

JD: Like getting together with actors and spending an evening reading a play. Going to the Lincoln Center Library every two weeks and taking out albums of two musicals you never heard before. Getting together with a friend who plays the piano—and maybe even with a bunch of friends—and just singing through music. Going to the movie musicals that play the revival houses.

Buying standing room for a Broadway show that you've seen already and seeing what has happened to it six months later, or seeing how the replacements are doing. I learned a great deal when I would go to see shows many times and see replacements and see how many different ways there are to approach a character. To see every single lady play Dolly was very instructive. There's no one way. When I sold orange drinks at the Shubert Theatre when *Promises, Promises* was playing, I saw over a long period of time what happened to the performances. Jerry Orbach was able to keep his performance absolutely fresh every night; other people were not quite as good at it. To see where the laughs came with different houses. To keep learning and growing is so important. That's what you do in between jobs. Just because nobody's paying you to work doesn't mean you stop working. Go to dance classes. Do those auditions. Try to keep yourself happy. Because if you're depressed and go into an audition depressed, it's going to show. Nobody wants to hire anyone who's desperate.

At the end of *The Count of Monte Cristo* by Alexandre Dumas is a wonderful quote, which reads:

> The Count just told us that all human wisdom was contained in these two words: wait and hope.

Show business is a lot like that.

APPENDIX F

ADVICE TO THE PERSONAL ACCOMPANIST

Please remember that you are there as an accompanist. You are not auditioning—or rather, you *shouldn't* be auditioning at the same time as the person who brought you.

This may sound strange, but *sensational piano playing at an audition is distracting. The attention and focus must be placed squarely on the singer.* Keep your accompaniments simple, straightforward, and supportive, and you will be doing your job well.

If the audition atmosphere is relaxed enough to permit some dialogue between the singer and the director, it is customary for the singer to introduce you; otherwise, you usually remain nameless. It comes with the territory.

However, if you hear that a piano job is available on the show, it is permissible to let your interest be known by giving your resume to the stage manager, or whoever is checking people in at the audition. If they are interested, they will get in touch and arrange for you to audition for the proper people.

APPENDIX G

HELPFUL NAMES AND ADDRESSES

The first—and best—place to look for names and addresses of book, record, and sheet-music stores is in your local Yellow Pages under the headings "Book Dlrs.," "Records-Phonograph-Retail," and "Sheet Music," respectively. Music copyists can either be found through your city's local chapter of the musician's union—American Federation of Musicians, or A.F. of M.—or through the music department of a university. Pianists can be located through the latter as well. Remember that the musician's union cannot recommend a certain music copyist over another, but they can provide you with a list of those available in your area.

In cities with a substantial theatrical industry, such as New York, Los Angeles, and London, there are a number of related businesses prepared to serve the trade knowledgeably. What follows is a workable but incomplete listing of some of the larger, more established firms that you could contact for assistance by phone, by mail, or, if it is a retail store, in person.

MUSIC PREPARATION—NEW YORK CITY

Associated Music — Copy Service
333 West 52 Street
New York, NY 10019
(212) 265-2400
Duplicating and copyist services provided, as well as music
paper and supplies.

ABC Music Reproduction Service
1633 Broadway
New York, NY 10036
(212) 583-9334
Services include music reproduction.

Chelsea Music Service
311 West 43 Street
Suite 1407
New York, NY 10036
(212) 541-8656
Copyists and music reproduction service provided.

Ideal Reproduction Company
1697 Broadway
New York, NY 10019
(212) 581-7355
Copyists and music reproduction service provided.

King Brand Music Papers
333 West 52 Street
New York, NY 10019
(212) 246-0488
Provides music reproduction service, as well as music paper
and supplies.

Music Preparation International
1697 Broadway
New York, NY 10019

(212) 586-2140
Provides copyists and music reproduction service.

MUSIC PREPARATION—LOS ANGELES

Alpheus Music Corporation
1433 North Cole Place
Hollywood, CA 90028
(213) 466-1371
Provides music reproduction service, as well as music paper
and supplies.

Bob Bornstein
c/o Paramount Pictures Music Library
5555 Melrose Avenue
Hollywood, CA 90038
(213) 468-5000
Provides copyist services.

Judy Green Music
1634 Cahuenga Boulevard
Hollywood, CA 90028
(213) 466-2491
Provides music reproduction services, as well as music paper
and supplies.

Bill Hughes
1251 Vine Street
Los Angeles, CA 90038
(213) 462-8390
Provides copyist and music reproduction services.

Joann Kane
14110 Valley Vista
Sherman Oaks, CA 91423
(213) 906-1325
Provides copyist services.

Pacific Music Papers
1305 North Highland Avenue
Hollywood, CA 90028
(213) 462-7257
Provides music reproduction services, as well as music paper
and supplies.

SHEET MUSIC—NEW YORK CITY

Colony Music
1619 Broadway
New York, NY 10019
(212) 265-2050
They stock a large selection of current in-print sheet music
and occasionally have some out-of-print oddities. They also
have a huge selection of phonograph records, both in-print
and out-of-print.

Music Exchange
151 West 46 Street
New York, NY 10036
(212) 354-5858
They stock a large selection of out-of-print sheet music.

BOOK STORES—NEW YORK CITY

Earlier in this book I mentioned the importance of becom-
ing familiar with the standard repertory of the music theatre.
Many musicals have had their scripts published and are therefore
available to read and study. First, try your local library. Then, try
the following book stores—again, an incomplete list:

Actor's Heritage
262 West 44 Street
New York, NY 10036
(212) 944-7490

Applause Theatre Books
211 West 71 Street
New York, NY 10023
(212) 496-7511

Coliseum Books
1771 Broadway
New York, NY 10019
(212) 757-8381

Drama Book Shop
723 Seventh Avenue
New York, NY 10019
(212) 944-0595

Theatre Arts Bookstore
405 West 42 Street
New York, NY 10036
(212) 564-0402

Theatrebooks
1600 Broadway
Room 1009
New York, NY 10036
(212) 757-2834

BOOKSTORES—LOS ANGELES

Larry Edmunds Bookshop
6658 Hollywood Boulevard
Hollywood, CA 90028
(213) 463-3273

Samuel French
7623 Sunset Boulevard
Los Angeles, CA 90046
(213) 876-0570

The book *Non-Equity Performer's SUMMER THEATRE GUIDE from an Actor's Viewpoint,* by John Allen can be ordered directly from Mr. Allen at P.O. Box 2129, New York, NY 10185.

BOOKSTORES—LONDON

Dillons
1 Malet Street
London WC1E 7JB

W & G Foyles Ltd.
113–119 Charing Cross Road
London WC2H OEB

Samuel French, Ltd.
52 Fitzroy Street
London W1P 6JR
England

PHONOGRAPH RECORDS—NEW YORK

Music Masters
25 West 43 Street
New York, NY 10036
(212) 840-1958

Painted Smiles Record Company
74–09 37 Avenue
Room 420
Jackson Heights, NY 11372
(718) 898-6964

Note: Both the above companies sell their records directly through the mail. Write or phone for catalogs.

PHONOGRAPH RECORDS (RARE)—LONDON

Dress Circle
57–59 Monmouth Street
Upper St. Martins Lane
London WC2H 9DG

LAGNIAPPE

MY FAVORITE AUDITION STORY

Once upon a time, a pretty young woman approached the piano and gave me her music. It was the vocally demanding coloratura aria "Glitter And Be Gay" from *Candide,* by Leonard Bernstein and Richard Wilbur. A six-minute number containing many passages that push the abilities of even the most accomplished sopranos to their limits, it builds to a vocally demanding high E-flat—the fourth note from the end.

Incredulously, I asked her, "Are you planning to sing the whole song?"

"Yes," she replied, "why, can't you play it?"

"Of course I can," I said.

She was halfway to the stage when she hurriedly came back to me and said, "I forgot to tell you—when we get to the ending, transpose it down a third."

ABOUT THE AUTHOR

Donald Oliver is an author and composer. He has compiled and edited the acclaimed collection of George S. Kaufman's writings entitled *By George,* and *The Greatest Revue Sketches,* a collection of fifty-seven short comic playlets culled from Broadway's most famous revues. He began writing musical comedies when he was in the eighth grade and later collaborated on several original musicals, which were produced at Tulane University. After graduation, he returned to his native New York, became a member of Lehman Engel's BMI workshop, and landed his first professional stint as an audition pianist for the Broadway show *Molly,* with Kaye Ballard. During the day, he taught music to children at the Dalton School, and at night found time to become artistic director of the Octagon Theatre Company, for which he co-produced well-received revivals of a number of musicals, including *Drat! The Cat!, Zorba,* and *Knickerbocker Holiday.* He was back on Broadway with the Marilyn Chambers show *Le Bellybutton,* and then became the music coordinator for the Alpha Team project of The American Dance Machine. Two of the happiest summers of his life were spent playing the piano for the tours of *Gypsy,* which starred Angela Lansbury. He was musical director for an intimate revue presented at Lincoln Center called *2,* and conducted the music for the cast album of that show. Three original children's musicals for which he composed the music and coauthored the scripts have been published by Chappell Music and are frequently performed throughout the United States. Having studied at the Manhattan School of Music, he continues to compose and has written the scores for the musicals *Murder at the Vanities* (book by James Kirkwood, lyrics by David Spencer), and *The Case of the Dead Flamingo Dancer* (book and lyrics by Dan Butler).